BRAIN SNACKS

Fast Food
for
Your Mind

For Brad,   OCT '21
Best regards,
Karl

Karl Albrecht

Publication Metadata:

Brain Snacks: Fast Food for Your Mind

© 2015, Karl Albrecht. All rights reserved.

240 pp.

ISBN: 0-913351-33-4

EAN: 978-0913351338

EyeThink Books is an imprint of Karl Albrecht International.

Contact: Pubs@KarlAlbrecht.com

The "Front Matter" is in the Back

Most people just skip that stuff any way, so let's get right to work. If you get that far, you'll see the usual Introduction, the author's philosophical diatribe, etc. There's no preface, no table of contents and no index, because I want you to discover the various brain snacks in this book one by one.

Here's your first snack.

Selfies: So, What's New?

Selfies are nothing new. Artists have been painting self-portraits for centuries. There's a catch, though – that selfie of Rembrandt is not what he looked like. It's how he saw himself in a mirror – backwards. That bump on the left side of his nose was actually on the right.

Same for Van Gogh and all the others.

Try this with your smart phone. Take a selfie, flip it left-to-right, and send it to your friends. See how many of them spot the difference.

Or, send both versions and ask them to tell you which is the normal one and which is reversed.

Multi-Tasking: What's the Big Deal?

Kids today brag about multi-tasking. My neighbor, who's 83, says, "What's the big deal about multi-tasking? I've been doing it for years. I can sneeze, cough, belch, fart, and pee at the same time."

Partly Baked Idea (PBI) # 1: What Shall We Name the Baby?

These days, advertisers try to place their commercials in every conceivable spot where they might get attention. One popular strategy is to buy "naming rights" to some well-known public place such as a sport stadium, a racetrack, or a conference center.

The obvious extension of this, of course, is naming babies. If you need to build up a little extra cash flow, and you have a baby on the way, why not sell naming rights for your child?

Think of the possibilities: your kid will be telling everybody "My name is Verizon Williams," or "Hi, I'm Nabisco Jones." Or, "I'm Budweiser Barnes – you can call me 'Bud.'" All through their lives they'll be advertising their sponsors every time they answer a phone, send an email, sign a check, or fill out a form. They should get paid for it.

Come to think of it, why not sell the rights to the family name? You might be able to get a good package price. "Meet John and Mary Citibank, and the little Citibanks."

Or, maybe not . . .

How Big is a Blue Whale?

Big.

Really big.

Really, really, really big.

The blue whale (*Balaenoptera musculus*) is the largest existing creature on earth, and probably the heaviest animal that has ever existed.

A typical adult will grow to more than 100 feet long and weigh almost 200 tons. That outweighs the largest dinosaurs ever discovered by about two-to-one.

Blue whales cruise at about 12 miles per hour, and dash at speeds up to 30 miles per hour.

A blue whale's lung capacity is typically about 1300 gallons, equivalent to the gas tank capacity of over 100 passenger cars. When it exhales, it blows a spout up to 40 feet high.

With a heart about the size of a Volkswagen and weighing 1,000 pounds or more, its primary aortic vessel is over 9 inches in diameter.

The whale's tongue alone typically weighs as much as 3 tons. Opened fully, its mouth can hold about 100 tons of water – and prey. But despite its huge mouth volume, it typically can't swallow any one object much larger than a beach ball. It feeds almost entirely on *krill*, tiny sea creatures that it scoops up in huge quantities. One whale may consume as much as 4 tons of krill per day.

When feeding, a blue whale can dive more than 300 feet deep in pursuit of krill, and can stay down for as long as 10-20 minutes.

Blue whales can store over 90 percent of the energy they take in, stocking up fat for the long migrations to and from their breeding grounds.

A baby blue whale already weighs about 3 tons at birth – about the same as a full-grown hippopotamus, and it might be as long as 25 feet. That's by far the largest animal ever produced by live birth.

A blue whale mother typically produces over 100–150 gallons of milk per day to feed her calf. The calf will initially put on weight at the rate of about 200 pounds every 24 hours.

The mother continues to feed the baby for about 6 months, by which time it will have grown to double its size at birth.

A male blue whale has one of the smallest brains for its size of any animal – about 15 pounds – but the largest penis of any animal – up to 10 feet long.

"The three great requirements for a happy life are:
something to do, something to love, and something to hope for."

~ *Joseph Addison, British essayist*

3

Nitwitticisms # 1

"When more and more people are thrown out of work, unemployment results."
~ *U.S. President Calvin Coolidge*

"The vast majority of our imports come from outside the country."
~ *U.S. President George W. Bush*

"Outside of the killings, Washington has one of the lowest crime rates in the country."
~ *Mayor Marion Barry of Washington, D.C.*

Question: If you could live forever, would you – and why?
Answer: "I would not live forever, because we should not live forever, because if we were supposed to live forever, then we would live forever, but we cannot live forever, which is why I would not live forever."
~ *Miss Alabama, in 1994 Miss Universe contest*

"God's like, so cool. Think of the coolest person in your life. He made that person. And He's cooler than that."
~ *Actress Justine Bateman*

"Why is he not learning or leaning so but so little, with my help. How comes his past teachers have been passing him from grade to grade without the advancing or progressing academicly. I will like to know what is causing the mental blockage."
~ *Brooklyn, NY elementary school teacher's student evaluation*

"Up your bottoms."
~ *Chinese host, toasting American diplomats*

"Up yours, too."
~ *American diplomats, returning the toast*

Thinking About Thinking

Thomas Edison said,

"Five percent of people think.

Another ten percent think they think.

And the other eighty-five percent would sooner die than think."

(A bit harsh, maybe – or maybe not.)

George Bernard Shaw said,

"Most people only think a few times in their lives. I've made an international reputation for myself by thinking two or three times a week."

The British statesman Horace Walpole said,

"The world is a tragedy to those who feel, and a comedy to those who think."

Charles Kettering, the American inventor and automotive genius, said,

"Human beings are so constituted as to see what's wrong with a new idea, not what's right. To verify this, you have only to submit a new idea to a committee. They will obliterate 90 percent of rightness for the sake of 10 percent of wrongness. The possibility a new idea opens up are not recognized, because not one [person] in a thousand has imagination."

Albert Einstein said,

"I fear the day that technology will surpass our human interaction. The world will have a generation of idiots."

Tenzin Gyatso, the 14th Dalai Lama, said,

"Who can say which will more important in the end: landing on the moon, or understanding the human mind?"

Don't Dis' the King

2d   Two students in Thailand face up to **15 years in jail for insulting the royal family** after performing in a play that featured a fictional king and his adviser.
BBC News ↗

I'll bet Yul Brynner wouldn't have put up with it, either.

"Whatever extra money I ever got, I spent on books.
If there was any left over, I bought food."
~ *John Adams, 2nd U.S. President*

♫ "All My Files, Lord . . ."

I'm told that Japanese versions of Windows offer more polite error messages than the English versions. Apparently they prefer a *haiku* style, in the poetic three-line form.

Like these, for instance:

A file that big?
It might be very useful.
But now it is gone.

Yesterday it worked.
Today it is not working.
Windows is like that.

The Web site you seek
cannot be located
but endless others exist.

Chaos reigns within.
Reflect, repent, and reboot.
Order shall return.

ABORTED effort:
Close all that you have.
You ask way too much.

First snow, then silence.
This thousand dollar screen dies
so beautifully.

With searching comes loss
and the presence of absence:
"My Novel" not found.

Windows NT crashed.
I am the Blue Screen of Death.
No one hears your screams.

Stay the patient course.
Of little worth is your ire.
The network is down.

A crash reduces
your expensive computer
to a simple stone.

Three things are certain:
Death, taxes, and lost data.
You may guess which has occurred.

You step in the stream,
but the water has moved on.
This page is not here.

Having been erased,
The document you're seeking
Must now be retyped.

Rather than a beep
Or a rude error message,
These words: "File not found."

Serious error.
All shortcuts have disappeared.
Screen. Mind. Both are blank.

Have You Written Your Epitaph Yet?

If you haven't composed your epitaph yet, maybe it's time to get going on it. You wouldn't want to leave such an important message – what people might think about you for a hundred years or more – to a bunch of unqualified amateurs, would you? Lord knows what sentimental drivel or lame clichés they might inflict on you.

I'm still working on mine. I have it narrowed down to a half-dozen or so possibilities, and I'll be sure to pick the final one before I ascend to the next plane of existence.

Of course, there could be a problem with an epitaph: what if they cremate you instead of bury you? Do they put your epitaph on the urn that your ashes come in? Or, should you order a cemetery plot and a headstone, just to make sure people see your epitaph? These are important life questions, folks.

I thought it would be a nice service to my readers to offer a few thought-provoking examples, something to get y'all started thinking. Here are a few of my favorites.

Some of the biggest names in history had fairly simple and modest departing words. For example,

Will Shakespeare wrote his own epitaph, inscribed on the stone covering his crypt in the old Trinity Church, in his native town of Stratford Upon Avon (forgive the historical spelling):

GOOD FREND FOR JESUS SAKE FORBEARE,

TO DIGG THE DUST ENCLOASED HEARE!

BLEST BE THE MAN THAT SPARES THES STONES,

AND CURST BE HE THAT MOVES MY BONES.

8

Isaac Newton reposes in Westminster Abbey, one of the highest honors bestowed upon a native Englishman. Alexander Pope proposed a snappy epitaph, but the Abbey's top brass rejected it in favor of a more serious, mundane tribute. Pope wanted the stone to read:

NATURE AND NATURE'S LAWS LAY HID IN NIGHT:

GOD SAID, 'LET NEWTON BE!' AND ALL WAS LIGHT.

MARCH 20TH 1727

Sir Christopher Wren, the genius architect who masterminded much of the reconstruction of London after the great fire of 1666, rests in the magnificent St. Paul's Cathedral, considered by many to be the crowning achievement of his brilliant career. His epitaph, in Latin, says:

LECTOR, SI MONUMENTUM REQUIRIS, CIRCUMSPICE

(Reader, if you seek his monument, look around you.)

Thomas Jefferson, the third president of the United States, didn't bother to mention that honor in his epitaph. He mentioned only the three achievements of which he was most proud:

AUTHOR OF THE DECLARATION OF AMERICAN INDEPENDENCE

OF THE STATUTE OF VIRGINIA FOR RELIGIOUS FREEDOM

AND FATHER OF THE UNIVERSITY OF VIRGINIA

Ben Franklin, ever the self-effacing wry humorist, said modestly of himself:

THE BODY OF BENJAMIN FRANKLIN, PRINTER

(LIKE THE COVER OF AN OLD BOOK, ITS

CONTENTS WORN OUT, AND STRIPT OF ITS

LETTERING AND GILDING)

LIES HERE, FOOD FOR WORMS.

YET THE WORK ITSELF SHALL NOT BE LOST,

FOR IT WILL, AS HE BELIEVED,

APPEAR ONCE MORE IN A NEW

AND MORE BEAUTIFUL EDITION,

CORRECTED AND AMENDED BY ITS AUTHOR.

Edgar Allen Poe, one of America's most popular novelists and poets, was content with the final line of his most famous poem, "The Raven":

QUOTH THE RAVEN,

"NEVERMORE."

Some of the less famous left behind whimsical or ironic epitaphs, or – in some cases – were interred with inscriptions devised by others, some with a dark sense of humor, or perhaps little respect for the deceased.

In East Dalhousie Cemetery, Nova Scotia:

HERE LIES EZEKIAL AIKLE

AGE 102

THE GOOD DIE YOUNG

In Arizona's famous Boot Hill cemetery:

HERE LIES LESTER MOORE

FOUR SLUGS FROM A .44

NO LES, NO MORE.

In Ruidoso, New Mexico:

HERE LIES JOHNNY YEAST

PARDON ME FOR NOT RISING

In Nantucket, Massachusetts, Ezekiel Pease is buried with:

PEASE IS NOT HERE,

ONLY HIS POD

HE SHELLED OUT HIS PEAS

AND WENT TO HIS GOD

Auctioneer Jedediah Goodwin is remembered as:

JEDEDIAH GOODWIN

AUCTIONEER
BORN 1828
GOING!
GOING!!
GONE!!!
1876

A long-lived spinster in Scranton, Pennsylvania was remembered as (note the clever pun in the last line):

1787 – JONES – 1855
HERE LIE THE BONES OF SOPHIE JONES.
FOR HER DEATH HELD NO TERRORS.
SHE WAS BORN A MAID AND DIED A MAID.
NO HITS, NO RUNS, NO HEIRS.

A gentleman named Thorp, reportedly a miser who resented paying by the letter for a carved message, decided to save money. He settled for:

THORP'S CORPSE

Thomas Smith, an enterprising businessman from Annapolis, Maryland, was not one to miss a selling opportunity. On his wife's gravestone he carved:

HERE LIES JANE SMITH
WIFE OF THOMAS SMITH, MARBLE CUTTER
THIS MONUMENT ERECTED BY HER HUSBAND
AS A TRIBUTE TO HER MEMORY.
MONUMENTS OF THIS STYLE
ARE 250 DOLLARS.

Disgruntled heirs in Amsterdam, who had been neglected in the deceased's will, decided to dis' him with:

EFFEN NYT

(In English it means "Exactly Nothing.")

Martin Luther King, Jr., the legendary civil rights leader, invoked a verse from an old slave spiritual:

FREE AT LAST. FREE AT LAST.

THANK GOD ALMIGHTY

I'M FREE AT LAST.

Show business people seem to have a preference for the wisecrack as a parting message.

Rodney Dangerfield, the durable comedian who specialized in self-deprecating humor ("I don't get no respect"), parted with:

THERE GOES THE NEIGHBORHOOD

Merv Griffin, a long-serving veteran of the TV talk show format, reminded his stone's viewers:

I WILL NOT BE BACK AFTER THIS MESSAGE

Mel Blanc, the venerable and well-beloved voice of many cartoon characters such as Bugs Bunny, Porky Pig, and Elmer Fudd, signed off with his trademark line:

THAT'S ALL, FOLKS!

Favorite Lame Joke # 1

A man lay on his deathbed, minutes away from expiring. His faithful wife sat next to him, patiently holding his hand.

He managed to rouse himself one last time and said, "Carol, I'm sorry, but I have a confession to make. It's something I can't bear to take with me to the grave."

"What is it, dear?" she asked.

"Well – this is rather uncomfortable – I was unfaithful to you. I had an affair with my secretary."

"I know, dear," she replied.

"You do!?"

"Yes."

"Well, there was another time, too. I had sex several times with the woman who lived next to us in Seattle."

12

"I know, dear," his wife replied.

He gazed at her in astonishment.

"Well," he said, "there was one other time – a lot worse than those, I'm afraid. I even had sex with your sister."

His wife replied softly, "I know, dear."

"You knew about all of those times?" he said, his face showing his puzzlement.

"Yes, I knew."

"But, didn't it bother you?" he asked, incredulous.

"Well, yes, it did bother me," she said. "That's why I poisoned you."

Those "OTUS" People

A common abbreviation for referring to the U.S. President is "POTUS," meaning "President of the United States."

Some people refer to the Congress as "COTUS."

Some refer to the Supreme Court as "SCOTUS."

Some go so far as to refer to the President's wife – the First Lady – as "FLOTUS."

I suppose that makes the Presidential family dog "FIDOTUS."

The system will probably break down, however, if Americans elect a married woman as president. Would her husband be "FGOTUS" – "First Gentleman?" Doesn't sound right.

If they called him the "First Dude," he'd become "FIDOTUS" – but that's already taken if they have a dog.

If you come up with an acronym that sounds OK, you might get a medal.

"Are You Crazy" Department

A woman in London decided to part company with her imaginary friend, Bernard, after extensive treatment by a psychologist. She put Bernard, up for sale on eBay. She said she felt entitled to some form of compensation for giving him up.

Mental Jelly Beans # 1

Attributed to comedian Steven Wright:

- ❖ I went to a bookstore and asked the saleswoman, "Where's the self-help section?" She said if she told me, it would defeat the purpose.

- ❖ Are vegetarians allowed to eat animal crackers?

- ❖ Borrow money from a pessimist – they don't expect it back.

- ❖ If a mute swears in sign language, does his mother wash his hands with soap?

- ❖ If the police arrest a mime, do they tell him he has the right to remain silent?

- ❖ If you shoot a mime, do you have to use a silencer?

- ❖ If someone with multiple personalities threatens to kill himself, is it considered a hostage situation?

- ❖ Is there another word for synonym?

- ❖ What should you do if you see an endangered animal eating an endangered plant?

- ❖ What was the best thing *before* sliced bread?

"If everything seems like it's under control, you're just not going fast enough."
~ *Mario Andretti, legendary race car driver*

Factoids # 1

- ❖ A cat has 32 muscles in each ear, compared to only 6 for humans. Cats can also move their ears separately and independently.

- ❖ An ostrich's brain is about the size of a walnut – smaller than its eyeball.

- ❖ The giant squid (*Architeuthis dux*) has the largest eyes of any animal, the size of volleyballs.

- ❖ A dragonfly can outfly a helicopter; it can hover, rise, descend, and move laterally in all four directions – including backwards. With a top speed of 60 miles per hour, it would lose a race with a man-made helicopter, but could easily out-maneuver it at close quarters.

- ❖ A flea can jump 350 times its body length. That's equivalent to a human jumping the length of a football field.

- ❖ A decapitated cockroach can live for several weeks without its head, before it starves to death. They don't need their heads as much as other animals – such as humans – do. The roach's brain doesn't control breathing or blood circulation. They breathe through *spiracles*, or little holes in each body segment. Because cockroaches are *poikilotherms*, or cold-blooded animals, they need much less food than other animals do. They're one of the most ancient species still living, and some biologists believe they might be one of the only animals to survive a global nuclear war.

- ❖ Some lions mate 40–50 times a day. Females are usually in heat for only a few days at a time, and during that period they can mate with their partners several times per hour. Mating is a brief procedure, however, lasting only about one minute – similar, in that way, to some humans.

"No – After YOU"

What's the name of that little dance you do with a complete stranger you encounter, when the two of you repeatedly change course – in the same direction – to avoid colliding?

You're absent-mindedly wandering down the aisle of the supermarket, or turning the corner, and you meet someone coming the other way.

You waltz to your left, and he waltzes to his right – so you nearly collide again.

Then you cleverly decide to arabesque to the right, and she sashays to her left, and you nearly collide again.

Then you both laugh about it, somebody makes a funny remark, and somehow you cooperatively decide who goes where.

15

I think that little dance deserves a name: maybe the synchronized two-step, or the sincerity waltz?

Have your suggestions on my desk by Monday for extra credit.

Famous Bad Calls # 1

"They couldn't hit an elephant at this dist —"

~ *Last words of General John Sedgwick*, a Union army commander, disparaging the legendary marksmanship of Confederate snipers.

"There is not the slightest indication that nuclear energy will ever be obtainable. It would mean that the atom would have to be shattered at will."

~ *Albert Einstein, 1932*

"Forget it, Louis. No Civil War picture ever made a nickel."

~ *Irving Thalberg*, financial adviser to Hollywood producer Louis B. Mayer, who turned down the chance to film "Gone With the Wind"

"Gone With the Wind is going to be the biggest flop in Hollywood history. I'm just glad it'll be Clark Gable falling on his face, and not Gary Cooper."

~ *Actor Gary Cooper*, who turned down the leading male role in "Gone With the Wind"

"Television won't last, because people will soon get tired of staring at a plywood box every night."

~ *Darryl Zanuck*, movie producer at 20th Century Fox, 1946

"We will bury you – and you capitalists will sell us the shovels to do it with."

~ *Soviet Premier Nikita Khrushchev*, addressing Western ambassadors at the Polish embassy in Moscow

"We stand on the threshold of rocket mail."

~ *U.S. Postmaster General Arthur Summerfield*, serving during Eisenhower's administration. He believed missile technology would make it feasible to deliver mail between continents via ballistic missiles.

"I see no reason why anyone would want a computer in their home."
~ *Ken Olsen*, founder of Digital Equipment Corporation

"Reagan doesn't have that presidential look."
~ *United Artists executive*, rejecting Ronald Reagan as lead in the 1964 film "The Best Man"

"I give them a year."
~ *Ray Bloch*, musical director for "The Ed Sullivan Show," when the Beatles made their first live appearance on American television over 50 years ago.

Give Me a Sign . . .

"If at first you don't succeed, skydiving probably isn't for you."
~ *Anonymous*

Suicidal Twin Shoots Sister by Mistake

PBI # 2: A Wise Disguise?

People often refer to "blessings in disguise." "Well," they say, after their neighbor's house has been blown away by a tornado, "maybe it's actually a blessing in disguise." On the other hand, it seems like very few people ever say, "Maybe this is a curse in disguise." What's the ratio of disguised blessings to disguised curses?

The New Airline Fees

As part of the continuing trend toward "unbundling" airline services and charging individually for them, the International Air Transport Association (IATA) has released its recommended "menu model" of charges. Eventually, the plan is to swipe your credit card when you board, and add the various charges to your account as you incur them.

Here are some of the creative new ways the airlines will be "improving" their service to their customers.

- ❖ Reservation Fee: $10
- ❖ Reservation Change Fee: $100
- ❖ Refund Fee: $10 (But You Get No Money Back)
- ❖ Fuel Surcharge: $10
- ❖ Ground Maintenance Surcharge: $10
- ❖ Terrorist Suppression Surcharge: $25
- ❖ Seat Selection Fee: $10
- ❖ Non-Center Seat Charge: $25
- ❖ Extra Leg Room: $25
- ❖ No Screaming Child in Your Row: $25
- ❖ No Huge Fat Guy Beside You: $25
- ❖ First Checked Bag: $10
- ❖ Second Checked Bag: $50
- ❖ Additional Checked Bags: You Can't Afford It
- ❖ Priority Boarding Fee: $10
- ❖ Homespun Monologue by Captain: $5

- ❖ No Homespun Monologue by Captain: $10
- ❖ Seat Belt Surcharge: $1
- ❖ Taking Off Your Shoes: $1
- ❖ Cell Phone Use: $5
- ❖ Wi-Fi Access Charge: $5
- ❖ In-Flight Movie: $5
- ❖ Overhead Bin Charge: $5
- ❖ Seat Pocket Use Charge: $5
- ❖ Barf Bag Charge: $5
- ❖ Earphones: $2
- ❖ Pillow: $2
- ❖ Blanket: $2
- ❖ Drink of Water: $2
- ❖ Booze: $5
- ❖ Bag of Peanuts: $2
- ❖ Meal or Snack Charge: $10
- ❖ Rest Room Charge: $2
- ❖ Peeing in Your Seat: $50
- ❖ Smiles By Flight Attendant: $1 each
- ❖ Jokes By Flight Attendants: $5
- ❖ No Jokes By Flight Attendants: $10
- ❖ Feeling Up the Flight Attendant: $50 (plus tip)
- ❖ Oxygen Mask Charge: $10
- ❖ Emergency Slide Charge: $10
- ❖ Priority Debarkation Fee: $10
- ❖ Checked Bag Retrieval Fee: $10

The agency says there may be more charges coming along, as the imaginative airlines marketing departments think them up.

The Devil is in the Dictionary

The Devil's Dictionary is a charming little book, written many years ago by Ambrose Bierce, a satirist, essayist, storyteller, and all around wise-ass.

For years Bierce wrote a column for *The San Francisco Examiner.* He made a habit of including a cynical or ironic definition at the end of each column, expressing his admittedly pessimistic outlook on the human condition.

He eventually collected a batch of them and published them in the little book.

His home in the quiet Northern California town of St. Helena, on the edge of the Napa wine country, is now a charming guesthouse.

Here are a few of my favorites:

Acquaintance, n. A person you know well enough to borrow from, but not well enough to lend to. A degree of friendship called slight when its object is poor or obscure, and intimate when he is rich or famous.

Bore, n. A person who talks when you wish him to listen.

Brain, n. An apparatus with which we think that we think.

Cannon, n. An instrument used in the rectification of national boundaries.

Clairvoyant, n. A person, commonly a woman, who has the power of seeing that which is invisible to her patron – namely, that he is a blockhead.

Coward, n. One who, in a perilous emergency, thinks with his legs.

Defenceless, adj. Unable to attack.

Destiny, n. A tyrant's authority for crime and a fool's excuse for failure.

Diplomacy, n. The patriotic art of lying for one's country.

Egotist, n. A person of low taste, more interested in himself than in me.

Eulogy, n. Praise of a person who has either the advantages of wealth and power, or the consideration to be dead.

Faith, n. Belief without evidence, in what is told by one who speaks without knowledge, of things without parallel.

Litigation, n. A machine which you go into as a pig and come out of as a sausage.

Litigant, n. A person about to give up his skin for the hope of retaining his bones.

Miracle, n. An act or event out of the order of nature and unaccountable, as beating a normal hand of four kings and an ace with four aces and a king.

Pray, v. To ask that the laws of the universe be annulled in behalf of a single petitioner, confessedly unworthy.

War, n. God's way of teaching Americans geography.

Have You Written Your Obituary Yet?

Surely you're not willing to have your obituary drafted by the same incompetent people who might have written your epitaph (if I hadn't reminded you to do your own)?

Your obituary can be as important as your epitaph. It lets people know you've taken on a whole bunch of saintly character traits you didn't have when you were alive. This is called the Post-Mortem Sainthood Effect.

People will cut it out, scan it, email it, frame it, and some might keep it forever. So consider the obit your chance to really tell your story – to let people know what a great person you were.

People who read obits tend to believe whatever they see. So, you can jack it up a bit. Don't put in a bunch of lies that they could easily debunk on the Internet, but definitely be your own PR agent.

You're entitled to all the buzz you can get.

"If you want to be sure of hitting the target,

shoot first, and whatever you hit, call that the target."

~ *Anonymous*

Better Than the King James Version

Here are some of the explanations attributed to children in Catholic schools, when asked to tell what they knew about the Bible stories.

> ➤ In the first book of the bible, guinessis, God got tired of creating the world so he took the sabbath off.

> ➤ Adam and eve were created from an apple tree. Noah's wife was joan of ark. Noah built and ark and the animals came on in pears.

> ➤ Lots wife was a pillar of salt during the day, but a ball of fire during the night.

> ➤ The jews were a proud people and throughout history they had trouble with unsympathetic genitals.

> ➤ Sampson was a strongman who let himself be led astray by a jezebel like delilah.

> ➤ Samson slayed the philistines with the axe of the apostles.

> ➤ Moses led the jews to the red sea where they made unleavened bread which is bread without any ingredients.

> ➤ The egyptians were all drowned in the dessert. Afterwards, moses went up to mount cyanide to get the ten commandments.

> ➤ The first commandments was when eve told adam to eat the apple.

> ➤ The seventh commandment is thou shalt not admit adultery.

> ➤ Moses died before he ever reached canada. Then joshua led the hebrews in the battle of geritol.

- The greatest miricle in the bible is when joshua told his son to stand still and he obeyed him.
- David was a hebrew king who was skilled at playing the liar. He fought the finkelsteins, a race of people who lived in biblical times.
- Solomon, one of davids sons, had 300 wives and 700 porcupines.
- When mary heard she was the mother of jesus, she sang the magna carta.
- When the three wise guys from the east side arrived they found jesus in the manager.
- Jesus was born because mary had an immaculate contraption.
- St. John the blacksmith dumped water on his head.
- Jesus enunciated the golden rule, which says to do unto others before they do one to you. He also explained a man doth not live by sweat alone.
- It was a miricle when jesus rose from the dead and managed to get the tombstone off the entrance.
- The people who followed the lord were called the 12 decibels.
- The epistels were the wives of the apostles.
- One of the oppossums was st. Matthew who was also a taximan.
- St. Paul cavorted to christianity, he preached holy acrimony which is another name for marraige.
- Christians have only one spouse. This is called monotony.

"Oh, the comfort –

the inexpressible comfort of feeling safe with a person;

having neither to weigh thoughts nor measure words,

but pouring them all right out, just as they are,

chaff and grain together;

certain that a faithful hand will take and sift them,

keep what is worth keeping,

and then, with the breath of kindness, blow the rest away."

~ *Variously attributed*

✪ ✪ ✪ ✪ ✪

Be Careful What You Wish For

If a magic genie would grant me only one wish, I think it might be that I would never again drop anything, misplace anything, or lose anything.

How satisfying that would be. It might be worth more than getting a whole bunch of money.

Or, maybe not . . .

Can You Solve This Famous Anagram?

Anagrams are those word puzzles that present themselves as scrambled arrangements of letters, often looking like real words, but not quite. Your task is to rearrange the letters to form the original word.

One of the most famous, and most tricky anagrams is:

teralbay

Legend has it that the Duke of Marlborough posed it to Queen Victoria, and she stayed awake for a whole night trying to solve it.

Give it a try – see if you can rearrange the letters to make a valid word. The answer, in the next paragraph, is encoded so you won't spot it before you've made a good try at solving the anagram.

Answer: numbering the letters of the alphabet from 1 to 26, and using each letter's numbered position instead of the letter (e.g. 1=a, 2=b, etc.), the spelling of the original word is 2-5-20-18-1-25-1-12. Substitute the letters for their matching numbers to see the answer.

Anagrams are often hard to solve because our brains lock into the existing pattern of letters, and it's difficult to break it up and try new ones.

A good trick for solving anagrams is to write each letter on a separate scrap of paper, lay them out in front of you, and keep scrambling them around until you spot a letter sequence you recognize.

Which Country Has the Most Camels?

Australia has more camels than any other country – by far – including African and Middle Eastern countries.

In fact, Australia in recent years has begun exporting camels and camel meat to other countries, particularly those with Islamic populations.

How could this have come about?

The answer emerges from an interesting historical event which, when connected with other events and trends, becomes perfectly clear. But without seeing the other elements of the story and the connections, the fact of Australia's role as the biggest exporter of camels would make little sense.

Here's the story that connects the dots.

The first settlers reportedly brought camels to Australia from the Canary Islands in 1840. Australia was a very large and sparsely populated continent, and it still is. The early settlers needed animals for transportation and carrying cargo over long distances, and camels provided an excellent option. They were strong, sturdy, durable, resistant to most diseases, and they were fairly easy to domesticate.

Historians estimate that more than 10,000 camels were imported, from as far away as Palestine and India, up until the turn of the twentieth century. Most of them were the one-hump dromedary variety. Camel farms sprang up to breed and sell them all over Australia, particularly in the "outback," the remote rural areas.

But by about 1920, when motor vehicles became widely available in the farther reaches of the bush, demand for the camels nearly disappeared. Their owners released thousands of them into the countryside, to wander freely. They continued to breed, of course, and having no natural predators, their numbers grew to an estimated 200,000 to 300,000 by the turn of the twenty-first century. These days, some experts estimate that the fluctuating camel population might outnumber Australian citizens by as much as two to one.

So now, after nearly a century, camels are a business again. Camel hunters, abattoirs, and exporters are capturing and slaughtering them, or loading them onto ships and sending them live to countries all over the world. They're abundant and cheap, and the export trade may not even be sufficient to keep their numbers under control.

Cell Phone Hygiene

Have you ever been in a public restroom – like in a restaurant, a department store, or a supermarket – and heard someone inside the toilet stall talking on his or her cell phone?

Does that give you the creeps? Somehow, those two activities don't seem to go together.

Can a person be so addicted, dependent, or fascinated with this modern electronic leash that they can't be away from it even long enough to take a ****?

If I were talking to someone who was on a cell phone, and I realized they were in a public toilet sitting on the throne, I think I'd instinctively hang up. E-e-e-e-u-u-u-w-w!!! Seems unsanitary. Could germs spread that way?

I guess not . . .

If George Washington Were Here . . .

Most people don't seem to know that George Washington wrote a book – well, almost a book. He compiled *Rules of Civility & Decent Behavior in Company and Conversation* during his school days in

Virginia, by copying a list of behavioral guidelines from the 16-th century French Jesuits. It's a useful little book – still in print, and easily available online. The 110 rules included advice on manners, conversation, how to dress, how to behave at meals, and general politeness and etiquette.

The book never made him famous as an author – he had a very different destiny – but over the years it has caused many students of history to reflect on his character, his upbringing, his times, and his personal philosophy. Some examples of George's rules:

2nd *When in Company, put not your Hands to any Part of the Body, not usually Discovered.*

38th *In visiting the Sick, do not Presently play the Physician if you be not Knowing therein.*

71st *Gaze not on the marks or blemishes of Others and ask not how they came.*

98th *Drink not nor talk with your mouth full; neither gaze about you while you are drinking.*

Your assignment: look up the rest of them and teach them to your kids.

"Though your talent be average – or less –
Use it anyway.
The world would be very silent
if no bird sang except the very best."
~ *Unknown Source*

PBI # 3: Where's My Book?

I keep hearing people use the expression "In my book . . ." to express their view of something. What is this "book" that everybody supposedly has? I've looked everywhere and I can't seem to find mine. Where do you get one? What's actually in it? Are they supposed to give you one when you're born? And is it the same one with all those tricks in it?

Cleopatra Was Not Egyptian

Here's a curious factoid that explains quite a bit of history in one little blurb.

Cleopatra VII, the last (acting) pharaoh of Egypt, was not an Egyptian – she was a pure-blooded Greek-Macedonian.

She was the umpteenth great-granddaughter of a military general named Ptolemy, who had been sent by Alexander the Great to rule over Egypt after he had conquered it.

The Ptolemaic dynasty ruled Egypt for nearly 300 years, from 323 BC to 30 BC.

During all that time, it was their practice to intermarry, rather than marry with Egyptians. In fact, many historians believe that Cleo followed that policy and married her brother.

She was quite a gal, and well worth reading about.

Egyptian Women Lost Something Along the Way

Though they may have been publicly and socially viewed as inferior to men, Egyptian women in ancient times had a great deal of legal and financial independence.

They could buy and sell property, serve on juries, make wills and even enter into legal contracts.

Egyptian women did not typically work outside the home, but those who did usually received equal pay for doing the same jobs as men.

Unlike the women of ancient Greece, who were pretty much owned by their husbands, Egyptian women also had the right to divorce and remarry. Egyptian couples were even known to negotiate an ancient prenuptial agreement.

These contracts listed all the property and wealth the woman had brought into the marriage and guaranteed that she would be compensated for it in the event of a divorce.

Question: where along the way did they lose their grip, and let men take over? Modern feminists would like to know.

Undoing the American Revolution

English comedian and satirist John Cleese finally got fed up with the craziness he was observing in America, and decided to set things right. He sent a message to Americans, explaining what was going to happen, and reminding them they'd brought it on themselves, and that it was for their own good.

Dear Americans:

In light of your failure to elect a competent president of the USA and thus to govern yourselves, we hereby give notice of the revocation of your independence, effective immediately. Her Sovereign Majesty Queen Elizabeth II will resume monarchical duties over all states, commonwealths, and territories (excepting Kansas, which she does not fancy).

Your new prime minister, Tony Blair, will appoint a governor for America without the need for further elections. Congress and the Senate will be disbanded. A questionnaire may be circulated next year to determine whether any of you noticed.

To aid in the transition to a British Crown Dependency, the following rules are introduced with immediate effect:

1. You should look up "revocation" in the Oxford English Dictionary.

2. Then look up "aluminium," and check the pronunciation guide. You will be amazed at just how wrongly you have been pronouncing it.

3. The letter "u" will be reinstated in words such as "favour" and "neighbour." Likewise, you will learn to spell "doughnut" without skipping half the letters, and the suffix "-ize" will be replaced by the suffix "-ise." Generally, you will be expected to raise your vocabulary to acceptable levels. (look up "vocabulary").

4. Using the same twenty-seven words interspersed with filler noises such as "like" and "you know" is an unacceptable and inefficient form of communication. There is no such thing as U.S. English. We will let Microsoft know

on your behalf. The Microsoft spell-checker will be adjusted to take account of the reinstated letter "u" and the elimination of "-ize." You will relearn your original national anthem, "God Save the Queen."

5. July 4th will no longer be celebrated as a holiday.

6. You will learn to resolve personal issues without using guns, lawyers, or therapists. The fact that you need so many lawyers and therapists shows that you're not adult enough to be independent. Guns should only be handled by adults. If you're not adult enough to sort things out without suing someone or speaking to a therapist, then you're not grown up enough to handle a gun.

7. Therefore, you will no longer be allowed to own or carry anything more dangerous than a vegetable peeler. A permit will be required if you wish to carry a vegetable peeler in public.

8. All American cars are hereby banned. They are crap and this is for your own good. When we show you German cars, you will understand what we mean.

9. All intersections will be replaced with roundabouts, and you will start driving on the left with immediate effect. At the same time, you will go metric with immediate effect and without the benefit of conversion tables. Both roundabouts and metrication will help you understand the British sense of humour.

10. The Former USA will adopt UK prices on petrol (which you have been calling gasoline) – roughly $6/U.S. gallon. Get used to it.

11. You will learn to make real chips. Those things you call French fries are not real chips, and those things you insist on calling potato chips are properly called crisps. Real chips are thick cut, fried in animal fat, and dressed not with catsup but with vinegar.

12. The cold tasteless stuff you insist on calling beer is not actually beer at all. Henceforth, only proper British Bitter will be referred to as beer, and European brews of known and accepted provenance will be referred to as Lager. American brands will be referred to as Near-Frozen Gnat's

Urine, so that all can be sold without risk of further confusion.

13. Hollywood will be required occasionally to cast English actors as good guys. Hollywood will also be required to cast English actors to play English characters. Watching Andie MacDowell attempt English dialogue in "Four Weddings and a Funeral" was an experience akin to having one's ears removed with a cheese grater.

14. You will cease playing American football. There is only one kind of proper football; you call it soccer. Those of you brave enough will, in time, be allowed to play rugby (which has some similarities to American football, but does not involve stopping for a rest every twenty seconds or wearing full kevlar body armour like a bunch of nancies).

15. Further, you will stop playing baseball. It is not reasonable to call an event the World Series for a game that is only played in America. Since only 21% of you are aware that there is a world beyond your borders, your error is understandable.

16. You must tell us who killed JFK. It's been driving us mad.

17. An internal revenue agent (i.e. tax collector) from Her Majesty's Government will be with you shortly to ensure the acquisition of all monies due (backdated to 1776).

18. Daily Tea Time begins promptly at 4 PM with proper cups, never mugs, with high quality biscuits (cookies, as you've been calling them) and cakes; strawberries when in season.

Thank you for your co-operation.

Signed (on Her Majesty's behalf),

~ John Cleese

"I distrust those people who know so well what God wants them to do, because I notice it always coincides with their own desires."

~ *Susan B. Anthony, American reformer and suffragist*

The Questionable Legend of Paul Revere

American school kids dutifully learn the story of Paul Revere, the New England silversmith and patriot who reportedly made a bold midnight ride to warn the good people of Lexington and the other communities north of Boston that "The British Are Coming!"

He almost certainly did make a ride, but he only became famous as a result of a historically inaccurate – and even manufactured – account in a poem by Henry Wadsworth Longfellow, over *85 years after the event*.

"Paul Revere's Ride" first appeared in the January 1861 issue of *The Atlantic Monthly*.

Revere had two fellow riders, William Dawes and Samuel Prescott. They ran into a British patrol while on their midnight mission. Dawes and Prescott escaped, but the British herded Revere back to Lexington and reportedly took away his horse, so he had to walk back to Boston. He never finished his famous ride.

Many years later, Longfellow invoked his right of poetic license and portrayed Revere as the only hero of the episode, implying that he had completed his mission. His creatively embellished poem manufactured the larger-than-life figure of Paul Revere known to American school children for over 100 years.

According to wikipedia.com,

> Revere's elevated historical importance also led to unsubstantiated rumors that he made a set of false teeth for George Washington. His legendary status continued for decades and, in part due to Longfellow's poem, authentic silverware made by Revere commanded high prices. Wall Street tycoon J. P. Morgan, for example, offered $100,000 for a punch bowl Revere made.

> The city of Boston erected a statue to Revere in 1883, but no significant memorials exist for William Dawes or Samuel Prescott.

A protest poem, written by Helen F. Moore in 1896, offered a parody of Longfellow's version:

'Tis all very well for the children to hear
Of the midnight ride of Paul Revere;

32

But why should my name be quite forgot,
Who rode as boldly and well, God wot?
Why should I ask? The reason is clear:
My name was Dawes and his Revere.

Clichés We Can Do Without

When the reporter pushes the mike in the face of the next of kin to a person killed as part of his occupation, the cliché answer is:

"He died doing what he loved."

✪ ✪ ✪ ✪ ✪

Nietzsche is Dead.
~ God

~~God is Dead.~~
~ ~~Nietzsche~~

✪ ✪ ✪ ✪ ✪

Curious Contradictions

Pardon me for saying, but I can't remember ever looking in the door of a "beauty parlor" and seeing a beautiful woman working there. In fact, they seem remarkably unbeautiful. Just sayin' . . .

I've also met a fair number of teachers who, it seemed to me, actually hate kids. Maybe they started out loving them, and maybe the kids slowly drove them crazy over the years. Just a guess . . .

I've also met some psychologists, psychiatrists, and therapists who weren't wrapped too tight. Maybe the "helping professions" attract people who need help?

Or, maybe not . . .

"It is not enough to be busy; so are the ants.

The question is: what are we busy about?"

~ Richard Bach, American inspirational author

Customer Service? Who Needs That?

While waiting in an Amtrak station for a friend to arrive, I noticed a sign prominently displayed on the counter. It said,

"Tickets will not be sold within five minutes of departure."

The policy certainly seemed reasonable, I suppose. They shouldn't have to delay the train just for somebody who dashes in right at departure time waving a credit card.

But on second thought, the sign seemed vaguely unfriendly.

Maybe they could have made it a more customer-friendly message by changing it to:

"We sell tickets up to five minutes before departure."

Seems like a small semantic distinction, but it seems to me to convey a more cooperative, less authoritarian tone.

Not to single out the train company – I see these kinds of ill-considered customer messages just about everywhere.

"There is no problem in this world that can't be made better by a donut."

~ Roseanne Barr, American comedian

Cynical Advice, But Maybe Worth Considering

"Men have died from time to time, and worms have eaten them, but not for love."

~ William Shakespeare

"Love is an ideal thing. Marriage is real. Confusing the real with the ideal never goes unpunished."

~ *J. W. von Goethe, German philosopher*

"Never do card tricks for the people you play poker with."

~ *Anonymous*

"In modern war there is nothing sweet nor fitting in your dying. You will die like a dog and for no good reason."

~ *Ernest Hemingway, American novelist*

"Always look for the fool in the deal. If you don't see one, it's you."

~ *Anonymous*

"If anyone is going to stab you in the back, it'll be someone you trust; you'll be watching your enemies."

~ *Anonymous*

"And if you're doing a deal with a religious son of a bitch, get it in writing."

~ *William S. Burroughs, American novelist*

"The next time I start thinking about getting married, I'll just find a woman I don't like and give her a house."

~ *Rod Stewart, rock singer*

"Every time you see a beautiful woman, just remember, somebody else got tired of putting up with her shit."

~ *Kinky Friedman, Texas writer and activist*

"Any American who is prepared to run for president should automatically, by definition, be disqualified from ever doing so."

~ *Gore Vidal, American novelist*

Outrageous Answers to Simple Questions

The long-gone TV show "Hollywood Squares" had various show-business people answering questions posed by a studio host. Some of the off-the-wall answers had the audience rolling:

Q. Paul, what is a good reason for pounding meat?
A. Paul Lynde: Loneliness!

Q. Do female frogs croak?
A. Paul Lynde: If you hold their little heads under water long enough.

Q. If you're going to make a parachute jump, at least how high should you be?
A. Charley Weaver: Two days of steady drinking ought to do it.

Q. True or False, a pea can last as long as 5,000 years?
A. George Gobel: Boy, it sure seems that way sometimes.

Q. You've been having trouble going to sleep. Are you probably a man or a woman?
A. Don Knotts: That's what's been keeping me awake.

Q. According to *Cosmopolitan*, if you meet a stranger at a party and you think that he is attractive, is it okay to come out and ask him if he's married?
A. Rose Marie: No, wait until morning.

Q. Which of your five senses tends to diminish as you get older?
A. Charley Weaver: My sense of decency.

Q. Charley, you've just decided to grow strawberries. Are you going to get any during the first year?
A. Charley Weaver: Of course not, I'm too busy growing strawberries.

Q. During a tornado, are you safer in the bedroom or in the closet?

A. Rose Marie: Unfortunately Peter, I'm always safe in the bedroom.

Q. Can boys join the Campfire Girls?
A. Marty Allen: Only after lights out.

Q. According to Ann Landers, is there anything wrong with getting into the habit of kissing a lot of people?
A. Charley Weaver: It got me out of the army.

Q. Back in the old days, when Great Grandpa put horseradish on his head, what was he trying to do?
A. George Gobel: Get it in his mouth.

Q. When a couple have a child, which of them is responsible for its sex?
A. Charley Weaver: I'll lend him the car, the rest is up to him.

Q. Jackie Gleason recently revealed that he firmly believes in them and has actually seen them on at least two occasions. What are they?
A. Charley Weaver: His feet.

PBI # 4: Seven Percent of What?

It's a common expression: "Well, we only use X percent of our brain's capacity." Sometimes it's "fifteen percent"; sometimes it's a more scientific-sounding "seven percent" or a similarly precise number. Here's an inconvenient question: how does anybody know what the brain's "capacity" is? Has someone measured it? What are the units of measure? Gigabytes? Gigahertz? RPM? Furlongs per fortnight? Could this be one of those popular slogans that fall apart when you think about them?

"We're all made of star stuff."
Carl Sagan, American astronomer, popularizer of science

Did He or Didn't He?

Whoever wrote this item for *The Week* magazine might have been a bit hung over, or otherwise intellectually impaired:

> *LGBT law*: Arkansas was poised this week to ban local governments from enacting laws that protect LGBT people from discrimination, after Governor Asa Hutchinson declined to veto the controversial legislation.

Huh?

The Romance of Olde England

Queen Elizabeth I, who reigned in Bill Shakespeare's day, must have seemed like a compulsive clean-freak to most of the people in her realm.

She reported bathed rather frequently, as often as twelve times per year.

Yeah – per year.

This was a time when the majority of people never bathed, and some of them bathed once a year, whether they needed it or not. I suppose a few of them got caught in a heavy rain now and then, or maybe they fell into a river or lake, but that was pretty much the extent of their hygiene.

Children typically had their clothes sewn onto them, to be cut away and discarded at the time of the annual bath.

For those who did bathe, according to historians, it was typically a family affair surrounding a barrel of water.

The man of the house would go first, then the adult sons, followed by the mother and the adult daughters. The kids came last.

According to historical accounts, they usually didn't bother to change the water during the process. By the time they had finished, the water was opaque with dirt and the surface was covered with the bodies of dead fleas and lice – even the nobility had 'em.

The last to get a bath were the toddlers and infants. Reportedly, that led to the expression "Don't throw out the baby with the bath water."

Just speculating, but I kind of doubt whether oral sex would have been a popular pastime in those days.

Deadlines and Taxes

Every year on April 15th – unless it's a Sunday – tens of thousands of Americans get into their cars just before midnight and rush to the main post office near where they live, to mail their tax returns before the deadline set by the IRS.

This seems like a strange ritual, considering that anyone can get a three-month extension of the filing deadline just by mailing in a request form. The extension doesn't have to be justified – it's automatically granted.

If they've already paid in more money than they expect to owe, they can file at their leisure. If not, they can mail in a check for some estimated amount.

Sure, they're eager to get their refunds, but they won't get them any faster if they mail the returns a few minutes – or a few days – after midnight.

The Postal Service has to stay open until midnight, and put on extra employees at overtime rates, to handle the deposits.

Seems like a big waste, and maybe an exercise in collective dumbness.

Favorite Lame Joke # 2

A young man met a good-looking older woman in a cocktail lounge, and they got into a pleasant conversation. She looked to be about 60-plus, but still very attractive.

After the conversation progressed, she boldly propositioned him with "Have you ever done a mother-daughter combo?"

"No," he replied, somewhat startled but definitely pleased. "I must say it sounds kind of interesting."

She invited him to her house. They walked in the front door, and she called upstairs:

"Mom? Are you awake?"

"The greatest obstacle to progress is not the absence of knowledge, but the illusion of knowledge."

~ *Daniel Boorstin, American historian*

✪ ✪ ✪ ✪ ✪

Dopey Definitions # 1

Arachnoleptic Fit, n. that frantic dance you perform just after you've accidentally walked through a spider web.

Bozone, n. The invisible substance surrounding ignorant people that stops intelligent ideas from penetrating.

Dopeler Effect, n. The tendency for dumb ideas to seem smarter when they come at you rapidly.

Foreploy, n. Any misrepresentation about yourself for the purpose of getting laid.

Glibido, n. All talk and no action.

Heebie-Jeebies, n. Irrational fear of Jewish people.

Intaxication, n. Euphoria at getting a tax refund, which lasts until you realize it was your money to start with.

Karmageddon, n. It's like, when everybody is sending off all these really bad vibes, right? And then, like, the Earth explodes and it's like, a serious bummer.

Reintarnation, n. Coming back to life as a hillbilly.

Sarchasm, n. The gulf between the author of sarcastic wit and the person who doesn't get it.

"Communicating with the dead is only a little more difficult than communicating with some of the living."

~ *Ashley Brilliant, American essayist, humorist*

✪ ✪ ✪ ✪ ✪

Reports of My Death are Greatly Exaggerated

> ### Karl Albrecht, a Founder of Aldi Stores, Dies at 94
> By DENNIS HEVESI and JACK EWING
>
> The German billionaire and his brother built their mother's World War II-era corner shop into a global grocery empire known for bare-bones ambience enlivened by cut-rate prices.

I'm not sure if I'm a descendent or relative of the German billionaire Karl Albrecht, but I sure do get a lot of his email by mistake.

At least two or three times a day I receive emails from people around the world, usually in developing countries, telling me how much they admire me and how happy they'll be if I'll just send them some money.

I would think that anybody who knows how to go to a website and find the email form there could also figure out that I'm an American management consultant and not the German billionaire Karl Albrecht.

I've been thinking about a reverse scam, maybe one in which they have to transfer some funds into a special account in order to qualify for financial assistance.

Wonder if it would work . . .

Speaking of Billionaires . . .

As of 2015, *Forbes* magazine reported the headcount for billionaires, worldwide, at 1,826. That includes 46 people younger than 40 years of age. Total net worth: estimated at $7 trillion.

Do You Love Chocolate? How Much?

According to *USA Today*'s scientific survey, the biggest consumers of chocolate in the world, ranked by average annual spending, are:

- ❖ Norway at $209
- ❖ Ireland at $182
- ❖ Switzerland at $172
- ❖ United Kingdom at $150
- ❖ Austria at $112

If you're American, you're barely in the top ten, at about $58.

Come on, Americans: where's your patriotism? Your national pride? Your sense of responsible consumption? Surely you can do better than that.

Proxemic Politics

Just after the Spanish Civil War (1936–1939), General Francisco Franco, who ruled Spain with an iron hand, commissioned the construction of an enormous cathedral, ostensibly to commemorate those who died in the conflict and to make his peace with the Vatican. "Celestial fire insurance," you know.

North of Madrid, the Valley of the Fallen features a 500-foot cross on top of a mountain, under which lies a huge basilica carved straight back into the granite face.

In a grand gesture of self-glorification, Franco planned for himself to be buried under the basilica, along with the leader of the defeated opposition party. In addition, some 40,000 of the one million soldiers who died during the civil war are also buried at the site.

After the basilica was completed – a twenty-year project that severely drained the government's treasury – the Vatican's representatives let it be known that it would not be eligible for consecration.

The reason for withholding consecration: the length of the basilica – the distance from the entrance to the back wall – was 252 meters (825 feet). That made it longer than St. Peter's Basilica in Rome.

To satisfy the Vatican representatives, the architects installed a false wall at the back, sealing off part of the length of the structure and making it shorter than St. Pete's.

Going Out In Style

I don't like to leave important matters to amateurs. That's why I'm going to plan my own funeral.

I mean, if it's the last big event associated with your time on Earth, why let other people screw it up? Why not do it in style, with some flair and some attitude?

First, we'll get all the sad stuff out of the way. The Scottish piper will lead everybody into the church playing "Amazing Grace." That always gets 'em crying, and makes 'em feel like they've been to a proper funeral.

Then I'll probably have an Irish comedian do the eulogy – but he'll be interrupted repeatedly with some innovative funeral stuff – recorded screams emanating from my casket; midget clowns running in to deliver my ashes in a coffee can; that sort of stuff.

Oh, and I definitely want 5 or 6 of those Arab women to come rushing in, wearing their black *chadors*, wailing, flailing, and beating themselves in grief. (You can hire 'em pretty cheaply these days.)

And forget those lame photo compilations transferred to video that you see at every funeral you go to these days. I'm going to shoot some original footage, and it'll wake 'em all up, for sure.

I don't have all the rest of it worked out yet, but I'd better get at it. Nothing worse than a half-assed funeral plan.

"O wad some pow'r the giftie gie us,

to see oursel's as 'ithers see us:

It would fra' monie a blunder free us,

and foolish notion."

~ *Robert Burns, Scottish poet*

PBI # 5: Who Said That?

Studies show that the most-often quoted philosopher is a Greek named Anonymous.

Gandhi Would Have Loved Our Beer

According to a news report:

> A Connecticut brewery apologized to Indians offended that the company is using Mohandas Gandhi's name and likeness on one of its beers.
>
> New England Brewing Co. sells an India pale ale it calls Gandhi-bot. The label features a cartoon image depicting a robot version of the late Indian leader, who favored prohibition.
>
> The brewery's website promoted the Gandhi-bot beer, which has been distributed for about five years, as "fully vegetarian" and "an ideal aid for self-purification and the seeking of truth and love."
>
> Gopalkrishna Gandhi, the spiritual guru's grandson, called the use of the image "crass and silly." Gandhi's great-grandson Tushar Gandhi, said that Gandhi "abhorred alcohol drinking and spoke against it."
>
> After a firestorm of outrage directed at the company's Facebook page, the firm posted an apologizing message that said, "We want to do our best to be culturally sensitive and respectful."

Yeah, right – only after they put a blowtorch to your backsides.

"You must be the change you wish to see in the world."
Mohandas Gandhi, Indian spiritual guru and civil rights leader

Sorry – Summer Has Been Canceled

Most people have heard about the great eruption of Mt. Vesuvius, the Italian volcano that buried the city of Pompeii in the year 79 CE. But that was like a firecracker compared to the biggest volcanic eruption ever observed.

In April 1815, Mount Tambora, on the Indonesian island of Sumbawa, blew its top so violently that it virtually shook the world. The explosion obliterated the top one-third of the 12,000-foot mountain, and set off a mind-boggling chain of events. One can only try to grasp the enormous scale of the energy released by the eruption, in terms of its immediate effects and its long-term impacts on global weather patterns.

Tens of thousands of people lost their lives in the immediate aftermath of the blow-up. The shock of the eruption created hurricane-force winds that wiped out villages on the neighboring islands, uprooted trees by the hundreds, and threw millions of tons of smoke and dust into the atmosphere. Chunks of pumice rained down for a radius of a hundred miles or more. Tsunami waves hit settlements a thousand miles or more away.

Observers all over the Pacific region reported bizarre weather effects for several months, including blackouts of the sun and strangely colored sunsets, caused by the massive amounts of volcanic debris circulating in the upper atmosphere.

By the following year, the atmospheric debris had spread across most of the globe, and it caused severe weather disturbances as far away as Europe. Through most of 1816, temperatures remained exceptionally low, contributing to widespread crop failures, sporadic famines, and even starvation.

Only decades later did scientists begin to fathom the total impact of the Tambora eruption, and 1816 became known as "the year without a summer."

"If dogs could talk, we'd probably have as much trouble getting along with them as we do with people."
~ *Karel Capek, Polish philosopher*

"America is the only nation in history that has gone directly from barbarism to decadence without the usual interval of civilization."
~ *Georges Clemenceau, French statesman*

Here's Your Political Bumper Sticker

If you're an American who likes to think, here's the only political bumper sticker you'll ever need:

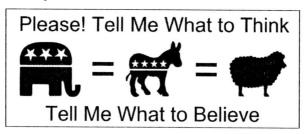

Download a printable version at: http://www.KarlAlbrecht.com/downloads/albrecht-bumpersticker-politicalparties.jpg.

Those Western Gunfights Were Quick and Clean

In those great old cowboy movies, the hero would meet the villain out in the street, man to man, and they'd shoot it out.

The bad dude would draw first, and our man would out-draw him. He'd pump off one perfectly placed shot and the other guy would drop, stone dead.

It looked great on the screen, but would anybody in his right mind fire just one shot and expect to kill somebody? While you were watching to see whether you got him with that one shot, he'd have time to shoot back if you missed. Common sense would dictate that you'd shoot several times, and maybe empty your gun on him.

A recent news story reported that New York's finest – their police, who train all the time – got into a shoot-out with a berserker on a crowded street. In the process of burning the guy down, four cops managed to shoot six by-standers.

Ah, those Hollywood guys – we can always count on them for an accurate portrayal of reality.

Did Sherlock Holmes Have Asperger's Syndrome?

"Mrs. Hudson, you're underfoot!"

Sherlock Holmes's long-suffering landlady and housekeeper often saw, at close range, how impatient, insensitive, inconsiderate, and indifferent he could be with people.

His obsessive interest in the craft of crime-solving crowded out almost everything else from his life, including the possibility of warm and reciprocal relationships.

His colleague Dr. John Watson was the only person privileged to share his personal space, with the possible exception of his brother Mycroft. And the relationship with Watson was bounded to that of wizard and apprentice.

His remarkable powers of observation, memory, relational thinking, and deduction made him a master of his craft, but he was famously incapable of relating to people as other than actors to be analyzed and explained.

These three core characteristics have led many to speculate that Sir Arthur Conan Doyle, his creator, had – more or less unconsciously – diagnosed him with what's now known as Asperger's Syndrome.

But wait – we're not talking about a real person here. Holmes was a fictional character, created for the amusement of Londoners in the late Victorian and early Edwardian periods. How can a fictional person be diagnosed with a developmental disorder?

To that, I say: So much has been written and said about him that he might as well have been a real person. We know more about Holmes the person than many real historical figures, including Queen Victoria. By analogy, even if Jesus Christ didn't actually exist, so much is recited about him that he might as well have.

People of the modern age, including to some extent those in England, usually don't appreciate the grand scope of Holmes's presence in England of the late 1800s and early 1900s. He was the Elvis Presley, the Michael Jackson, the James Bond, and the Arnold Schwarzenegger of his age, all rolled into one.

When Conan Doyle decided to kill him off in one of his episodes – which he serialized in London's *The Strand* newspaper – the public outcry and lament were deafening. None other than Queen Victoria wrote him a note urging him to bring Holmes back, almost as a patriotic obligation. He did.

And, judging by the pace of the conversations within and between the various Sherlock Holmes historical societies and fan clubs, he's as good as real. Their debates about the Asperger's question are ongoing and diverse.

My purpose here is not to join those debates. I won't mind if the question is never settled. But beyond the immediate question, I see a fascinating proposition: the best writers down through history may have taught us as much about human nature as our psychologists have.

In fiction writing, it's called "characterization" – the art of elaborating the psychological make-up of a person as a distinct, recognizable, and believable personality package.

Astute fiction writers, and even comedy writers, speak of a "character key," by which they mean a particular personality quirk, a flaw, a gift, an attitude, a driving purpose or value, or an unusual behavior that defines the character as unique and recognizable in the mind of the reader or viewer.

Holmes had two memorable character keys, each one needed to make the other believable: his keen, almost eerie power of observation, analysis, and deduction; and his utter indifference to the messy aspects of "human nature." Once the author builds the character, he or she uses these character keys to enable the reader to recognize and place the character within any given context. It's a cardinal sin amongst skilled authors to "mess with" a character once it's established.

So, how did Conan Doyle manage to craft this character over 100 years ago, considering that the Austrian psychiatrist Dr. Hans Asperger didn't show up to propose the syndrome until 1944?

Well, for starters, Conan Doyle had several of the elements of the character in his own experience, and possibly in his own head. He was a brilliant intellectual, educated at the University of Edinburgh, in Scotland. He became a physician, which placed him in frequent contact with the whole spectrum of normal and abnormal people.

And, he probably had a very useful role model, in his old university professor Joseph Bell. Conan Doyle reportedly wrote to Bell, "It is most certainly to you that I owe Sherlock Holmes. Round the centre of deduction and inference and observation which I have heard you inculcate I have tried to build up a man."

The wikipedia.org biography for Conan Doyle indicates that his old school mate Robert Louis Stevenson immediately recognized Bell as the character model for Holmes, as he read the stories in faraway Samoa.

Conan Doyle was also a super-achiever – a *polymath* – proficient in many sports, keen to travel the world, and willing to relocate in the service of his developing career. Holmes was often characterized as wiry, unusually strong, and agile when dire circumstances demanded it.

As a writer as well as a trained scientist, I often ask "Is fiction just fiction?" Is our knowledge of human beings limited to the truths we discover in research laboratories, or would we be better advised to think of all of life as the laboratory?

Sigmund Freud and Conan Doyle did their best work at about the same time. Which of those thinkers, and their intellectual descendants, have taught us more about people?

What to Do If You Think NSA is Reading Your Email

Humorist Andy Borowitz advises: just to stay on the good side of the surveillance people, try adding one or more of these little items to each of your email messages:

➢ I think the NSA is awesome.

➢ I just reread "Nineteen Eighty-Four" – it actually has some good ideas in it.

➢ There's no such thing as a "bad" drone.

➢ Sure am glad I never talk to any foreigners.

➢ The Fourth Amendment is overrated.

➢ If you ask me, Guantanamo is full of nothing but complainers.

➢ Just changed my Facebook status from "Single" to "In a Relationship with America."

➢ I'm pretty sure my neighbor is cheating on his taxes.

Jason Brings My Meal

When did the phrase, "You're welcome" get replaced by the phrase, "No problem"?

I haven't heard a waiter in a restaurant say, "You're welcome" in a long time, especially not a young one.

"No problem" sounds to me like it's discounting the value of the service just performed: it was no problem for Jason (or Britney, or whoever); He didn't have to go out of his way; didn't have to do anything special; it's nothing important.

On the other hand, "You're welcome" sounds like it's about me, not about the waiter's effortless procedure. He or she seems to be saying, "I appreciate you; what I've just done is especially for you."

Or, maybe not . . .

"Remember that silence is sometimes the best answer."

~ *Tenzin Gyatso, 14th Dalai Lama*

PBI # 6: War is Fun? Maybe

Maybe Union General William Tecumseh Sherman was mistaken when he famously declared, "War is hell."

War is only "hell" if you're one of the people getting maimed, killed, or driven out of your home. But if you're one of the heads of state, politicians, senior generals, diplomats, promoters, facilitators, arms makers, arms dealers, or suppliers of war materiel, war can be a lot of fun. If you're a president or a prime minister, it can keep you in your job.

Even if you're a soldier, it can be fun if you come back in one piece and have some great stories to tell.

If you're a reporter, you get to have fun writing stories about it.

If you're an historian, you get to write books about it.

If you're a college student, you get to protest it.

War has something in it for just about everybody – except the ones on the receiving end of it.

Maybe that's why we've had so much of it for so many centuries.

A Sadistic Scientist?

E.O. Wilson, a noted biologist, was curious about the way ants in a colony treated the ones that died.

In his research, he discovered a "death pheromone" – a chemical compound known as *oleic acid*, exuded by an ant's body just after it died.

He noticed that the other ants, apparently detecting the smell of the pheromone and taking that as evidence of death, would carry the corpse outside the nest and throw it into a sort of cemetery.

Curious to see whether he could fool the ants into thinking one of their number had died when it actually hadn't, he managed to synthesize the pheromone.

He caught one of the ants, put a dab of the synthetic pheromone on its body, and put it back into the population.

Sure enough, several of the other ants picked it up, dragged it kicking and screaming outside, and tossed it into the cemetery.

The disgruntled ant got up, indignantly brushed himself off, and went back into the nest. Right away, the other ants dragged him outside again and flung him into the cemetery.

One can only sympathize with the ant's plight, and imagine its reaction:

"Take your hands off me, you bastards! I'm not dead!"

"Yes, you are," they said. "We can tell by the smell."

"No, I'm not!"

"Yes, you are!"

Apparently, the poor ant was permanently banished from the colony.

It makes me wonder, was this an episode of science, or sadism?

Join Goodreads

Few activities will keep your mind in good condition and your inner world fresh more than reading.

Join Goodreads, which is an online community of over 30 million people who love the experience of reading, discussing, and sharing books.

You can join for free, set up your personal profile, get recommendations for new reads based on your expressed preferences, and link up with other people who have common interests.

Tell the good folks there that Karl Albrecht sent you (and be sure to post a flattering review of this book).

Reference: goodreads.com

God Loves the Beatles?

When asked what his research had led him to conclude about God, Chuck Darwin replied,

"Only an inordinate fondness for beetles."

Factoids # 2

❖ Winston Churchill was born in a ladies' room. His mother, an American who married into the Marlborough line, was big-time pregnant when she attended an upper-crust function at the luxurious Blenheim Palace. She went into labor unexpectedly and delivered in the powder room. Many Americans don't know Churchill was part Yankee.

❖ Al Capone's business card said he was a used furniture dealer.

❖ Alfred Hitchcock didn't have a bellybutton. Well, he actually did; it got covered over during one of several surgeries.

❖ Barbie's measurements, if she were life size, would be 39-23-33.

❖ Humphrey Bogart and Princess Diana were seventh cousins.

❖ Henry Ford, with all his money, never owned a Cadillac.

❖ Q: Who was the first American president born in a hospital? A: Jimmy Carter.

"...if we once start thinking, no one can guarantee
where we shall come out – except to say that
many ends, objects, and institutions are doomed.
Every thinker puts some portion of an apparently stable world
in peril,
and no one can wholly predict what will emerge in its place."
~ *John Dewey, American educator*

How to Stop a Show

Well before Viagra had come on the medical scene, Dr. Giles Skey Brindley, a British urologist, had been working on the idea of treating erectile dysfunction (a.k.a. impotence in those days) by injecting a compound called *papaverine*, also known as *phenoxybenzamine*, directly into the patient's penis.

Brindley was invited to present his findings at an evening keynote session at the Urodynamics Society conference, held in Las Vegas in 1983.

He met with a bit of skepticism from the audience about the effects of such a procedure, but he was well prepared to answer their questions. Immediately before the lecture, he had injected himself with the compound.

At a key moment in his presentation, he stepped out from behind the lectern. He opened his pants and displayed the result of his self-administered injection. The several hundred urologists attending the lecture went into pandemonium. Brindley walked around the lecture hall, inviting any and all to examine his penis to confirm that it was suitably erect.

He emphasized that the injected compound had a strictly chemical, hydraulic effect, rapidly dilating the blood vessels in the *corpus cavernosa*, the spongy chambers that fill with blood during erection. Reminding his audience of the absence of any normal erotic stimulus in the situation, he showed that his compound guaranteed results with no particular psychological involvement or sexual arousal at all.

The session became legendary amongst urologists and their allied professions, and many physicians began using the injections right away.

I've often pondered over the social impact of that event amongst the physicians themselves. If spouses were present, were they embarrassed by the offer, or possibly titillated? Suppose a police officer had been standing guard at the back of the lecture hall, perhaps serving as an off-duty private security guard. Would this be an incident of indecent exposure – indecent to whom? – and should he have arrested the doctor and hauled him away? Other such strange questions attach to the incident.

Some events can unravel our current construction of reality so thoroughly that we struggle temporarily, trying to put them back together. Some urologists say they still haven't fully recovered from the bizarre experience.

Last Words of the Dear Departed

"What were your husband's last words, before he died?"

"He said, 'Please put down the gun.'"

Little Frankensteins

I love to watch little kids when they're first learning to operate their bodies.

At the age of about one or two years, toddlers look like little Frankenstein monsters, staggering about, lurching from one place to another, with no two consecutive steps or movements the same.

I don't think "toddlers" is the right word for them.

It might be fun to dress 'em up – at least at Hallowe'en – to look like little monsters. After all, there are days when their parents and adult loved ones probably think of them that way.

They're not nearly as much fun for me to watch when they're older, because they're too "normal."

Crowdsourcing a Dictionary

Getting other people to do your work for you, and even raising money from crowds, is a popular activity in the Internet Age.

But that strategy goes back over 100 years – although without the benefit of cheap and rapid communication.

The *Oxford Dictionary of the English Language* was built by crowd sourcing, back in the nineteenth century.

Read a book titled *The Professor and the Madman: a Tale of Murder, Insanity, and the Making of the Oxford English Dictionary*, by Simon Winchester.

It tells the remarkable story of the project, and its most remarkable contributor, an American doctor named William C. Minor.

The work of compiling the Oxford Dictionary started in 1878, took 70 years to finish, and produced an inventory of 414,825 precise definitions.

The crowd sourcing method developed by the project's mastermind, Professor James Murray, involved asking everyone willing to contribute to scour through all the books they owned, write down all the words beginning with their assigned alphabetical letter or sequence of letters, and write a definition for each one on a separate slip of paper. Thousands of contributors mailed in their definitions from all over England.

Dr. Minor, a surgeon who had served in the U.S. Civil War and emigrated to England, contributed over 10,000 entries. Murray repeatedly invited him to visit Oxford to receive a commendation for his work, but Minor never went there.

Finally, in 1896, Murray decided to pay a surprise visit to Minor, in the town of Crowthorne, 50 miles north of Oxford. Arriving at the address he'd been given, he was astonished to find Minor locked up in Broadmoor, an asylum for the criminally insane.

It seems that Minor had experienced a psychotic episode shortly after coming to England, shooting to death a complete stranger on the street in London. He was incarcerated at Broadmoor for the rest of his life, mentally unstable but intellectually at the top of his game.

Reference: *The Professor and the Madman,* by Simon Winchester

It's Just Like Going to School

According to a psychologist friend of mine, "Living is like going to school. If you don't learn what you're supposed to learn, you get to take the course again."

Favorite Lame Joke # 3

Irish comedian Hal Roach loves to tell a story that he insists is typical of Irish humor, and maybe Irish people.

Murphy waited at the bus stop along a country road, and when the bus pulled up he leaned into the doorway and asked the driver,

"How much is the fare to Cork?"

"Four pounds," replied the driver.

"That's too much!" Murphy exclaimed. "I'm not for payin' that much."

"Please yerself," said the driver, and he drove off.

After a while, the driver happened to look into the rear mirror and he saw Murphy, running a few hundred yards behind the bus.

"Crazy bugger," he thought.

After about a mile, he came to another stop. He waited a few minutes until Murphy caught up, thinking he might have changed his mind.

"What's the fare to Cork, now?" gasped Murphy, nearly breathless and sweating from all that running.

"Five pounds," replied the driver.

"What?" demanded Murphy. "Back there you said the fare was four pounds."

"It was," replied the driver. "Ye been chasin' the wrong bus – Cork is in the other direction."

PBI # 7: Outsourcing War?

Business experts are fond of advising corporate executives to "outsource" – i.e. have somebody else do – everything but their "core competencies." This has led to a global shakeout as various business functions get outsourced to companies in countries that can do it cheaper, and sometimes better.

This leads to an intriguing proposition: all countries could outsource their war making efforts to the United States. After all, the U.S. is clearly the leading military force in the world, with the latest technology and the most highly trained, expert fighters. No other country makes war as well as the U.S. does.

If all countries outsourced their war making to the U.S., they could be sure of getting the best operations for their money. Where would this lead? For one thing, the country willing to put up the most money would always win, because both sides would be buying military operations of identical quality.

The drawback, one might say, would be that Americans would be fighting each other. But, if the best–funded side would always win, then Americans could simply scale down the battles to make sure the right sponsor won, but with minimum casualties – and higher profits.

In the end, maybe the wars could be fought with computers, and the losing side would have to pay money to the winning side. Maybe one soldier would have to get shot to make it a real war.

Would this work?

Masons in the White House

Fourteen U.S. presidents were confirmed members of the Freemasons. Several others have been involved with the Masonic organization, but not actually members.

The full members were:

- o   George Washington
- o   James Monroe
- o   Andrew Jackson
- o   James Knox Polk
- o   James Buchanan
- o   Andrew Johnson
- o   James Abram Garfield

- William McKinley
- Theodore Roosevelt
- William Howard Taft
- Warren Gamaliel Harding
- Franklin Delano Roosevelt
- Harry S. Truman
- Gerald Rudolph Ford

Three in a row were McKinley, Teddy Roosevelt, and Taft. Two in succession were FDR and Truman.

It seems very unusual that a relatively small sect like the Masons would have had almost one-third of all presidents as members. *Maybe there's a good conspiracy theory here?*

"Everything should be made as simple as possible, but not simpler."

~ Albert Einstein

Men Are Just Happier People

Men are probably happier than women, for one main reason: they keep things simple. If you're a man:

- Your last name stays put.
- The garage is all yours.
- Wedding plans take care of themselves.
- Chocolate is just another snack.
- You can be President.
- You can never be pregnant.
- Car mechanics tell you the truth.
- The world is your urinal. You never have to drive to another gas station restroom because this one is just too icky.

- You don't have to stop and think of which way to turn a nut on a bolt.
- Same work, more pay.
- Wrinkles add character.
- Wedding dress: $5000. Tux rental: $100.
- People never stare at your chest when you're talking to them.
- The occasional well-rendered belch is practically expected.
- New shoes don't cut, blister, or mangle your feet.
- One mood all the time.
- Phone conversations are over in 30 seconds flat.
- You know stuff about tanks.
- A five-day vacation requires only one suitcase.
- You can open all your own jars.
- You get extra credit for the slightest act of thoughtfulness.
- Your underwear is $8.95 for a three-pack. Three pairs of shoes are more than enough.
- You almost never have strap problems in public. You are unable to see wrinkles in your clothes.
- Everything on your face stays its original color. The same hairstyle lasts for years, maybe decades. You only have to shave your face and neck.
- You can play with toys all your life.
- One wallet and one pair of shoes – one color for all seasons.
- You can wear shorts no matter how your legs look.
- You can do your nails with a pocket knife.
- You have freedom of choice concerning growing a mustache.
- You can do Christmas shopping for 25 relatives on December 24 in 25 minutes.

No wonder men are happier.

Good News Travels Slowly

The Battle of New Orleans was the last major engagement of the War of 1812, between the U.S. and the invading British army.

The battle – which the American troops won – took place about three weeks after the peace treaty was signed.

Why did the fighting continue for so long?

Because it took that long for the news to travel from Ghent (where the signing took place, now in Belgium) back to Washington, and then to New Orleans.

Time scales like that seem so strange to modern humans, who get impatient if their email doesn't get through in a fraction of a second.

Try to imagine what life would have been like, unfolding at that kind of a pace.

✪ ✪ ✪ ✪ ✪

What if the hokey-pokey really is what it's all about?

✪ ✪ ✪ ✪ ✪

Are You a "Mental Redneck?"

American comedian Jeff Foxworthy draws upon his heritage as a child of the South, by inviting his listeners to consider whether "You might be a redneck." He poses various hypothetical behaviors to give his audience a "neck check."

> "If you have a complete set of salad bowls and they all say 'Cool-Whip' on the side," he advises, "you might be a redneck."

"If you're wearing a strapless dress and a bra that isn't, you could be a redneck."

"If more than three rooms in your house have talking fish mounted on the wall, you just might be a redneck."

"If you've been married three times and still have the same in-laws, you might be a redneck."

A redneck, in typical American usage, is an uncouth person of limited education – typically from the rural South – with an arrested social development, a narrow experience of culture and aesthetic experience, traditionalist attitudes and reactions, and self-indulgent preferences for experience. Stereotypical rednecks typically own guns, drive trucks or old rattle-trap cars, and like to fish and hunt.

Southerners in the U.S. also call them "bubbas." Australians call them "yabbos." In Hawai'i, they're known as "mokes."

They respond strongly to simple appeals such as patriotism or religious fundamentalism and take offense easily at perceived slights against the social or political groups they identify with. At their best, they are supposedly friendly, unassuming, and uncomplicated – "a glorious absence of sophistication," as Foxworthy affectionately describes them. At the extreme, a redneck is narrow-minded, bigoted, intolerant, boorish, and resentful of others who act "snooty."

Some people are "mental rednecks." They may not dress like stereotypical social rednecks, or even talk the way they talk, but nevertheless they think like rednecks. Mental redneck thinking is quite prevalent, including amongst supposedly "well-bred" people, who may have college educations, well-paying jobs, and comfortable living styles. It's a learned pattern of incompetence.

Mental redneck thinking is narrow, rigid, intolerant, resistant to change, unaccepting of other perspectives, and motivated by the need for simple answers and a comfortable sense of "law and order." Mental rednecks usually don't think of themselves as rednecks, of course. They typically like to think of themselves as having a firm grip on the problems and challenges of life, but paradoxically it's their fear of the loss of a sense of control, structure, and order – not having simple answers and simple solutions – that leads them to act out in ambiguity-avoiding patterns.

Mental redneck thinking is often selective: a person might think like a redneck on one topic, such as politics, and yet think more open-mindedly or creatively about others. People who are open to ideas in one area may snap into a reflexive, intolerant pattern of thinking when their hobby-horse topic comes up in conversation.

And, lest it go unstated, there are probably as many female rednecks as males – both mental and social.

The Mental Redneck Quiz

How do you know if you're a mental redneck? Taking a cue from comedian Foxworthy, here's a neck-check for the mind:

- ✓ If you get most of your information about the society you live in from watching television – you might be a mental redneck.

- ✓ If you take pride in having strong opinions and stoutly defending them, and you have no patience with wimps who don't – you could be a mental redneck.

- ✓ If you often say "I don't care what anybody says, that's my opinion" – you just might be a mental redneck.

- ✓ If you subscribe to three or more conspiracy theories about who's behind the bad things that are happening in the world today – you might be a mental redneck.

- ✓ If your car has more than one flag decal, religious bumper sticker, or political slogan – you could be a mental redneck.

- ✓ If you haven't been into a bookstore (or bought a book online) during the last year – you just might be a mental redneck.

- ✓ If the extent of your magazine reading is *People* magazine, *Cosmopolitan*, *Sports Illustrated*, or *Playboy* – you might be a mental redneck.

- ✓ If you know the names of all of the characters in the most popular TV shows but can't name the head of state of any foreign country – you could be a mental redneck.

- ✓ If you know more about the personal lives of movie stars, sports figures, or celebrity criminals than you know about the qualifications of the people you vote for – you just might be a mental redneck.

- ✓ If you vote for all the candidates on the ballot who belong to one political party – you just might be a mental redneck.

- ✓ If you emphatically claim "I don't vote for any party, I vote for the person" and then you go ahead and vote for all the candidates on the ballot who belong to one political party – you might be a mental redneck.

- ✓ If you get all of your ammunition for political debates with your friends and acquaintances from a talk show host – you could be a mental redneck.

- ✓ If you've reduced your views and judgments about social and political issues to a set of standard slogans, which you routinely trot out in conversations – you just might be a mental redneck.

- ✓ If you're convinced that anyone who doesn't embrace your particular religious beliefs is doomed to burn in hell – you might be a mental redneck.

- ✓ If you're convinced that anyone who doesn't embrace your particular political opinions is mentally incompetent, morally corrupt, or otherwise defective – you could be a mental redneck.

What's Your Mental Redneck Rating?

If you scored high on mental redneck-ism, maybe you like it that way. You might enjoy saying things like "I don't know anything about art, but I know what I like." You might enjoy arguing politics, armed with the latest talking points supplied by your favorite talk show host.

Or, maybe you'd like to broaden your mental world. You might want to open up to new ideas and new points of view; become more tolerant of the views and ideas of others; and expose yourself to new experiences that invite you to learn and grow.

Either way, the choice is entirely yours. You get to decide which way you want to grow.

Dopey Definitions # 2

Abdicate, v. To give up all hope of ever having a flat stomach.

Balderdash, n. A rapidly receding hairline.

Coffee, n. The person upon whom one coughs.

Esplanade, v. To attempt an explanation while drunk.

Flabbergasted, adj. Appalled by discovering how much weight you've gained.

Flatulance, n. The emergency vehicle that picks up someone who's been run over by a steamroller.

Vegetarian, n. A failed hunter.

Paradox, n. Two physicians.

Control, n. A short, ugly inmate.

Pokemon, n. A Jamaican proctologist.

"No problem can be solved from the same consciousness that created it. We must learn to see the world anew."
~ *Albert Einstein, noted theoretical scientist*

More Presidents Than We Need?

America had three presidents in the same year – 1841.

The 8th president, Martin Van Buren, finished his term on March 4th of that year.

William Henry Harrison took over as the elected 9th president on that day.

Harrison, however, died after only 32 days in office.

His vice president, John Tyler, succeeded him on April 4 and served out the remainder of the term.

It happened again, 40 years later.

In 1881, Rutherford B. Hayes, James A. Garfield, and Chester A. Arthur also occupied the White House during the same 12-month period.

Hayes completed his term; Garfield succeeded him, but died from gunshot wounds inflicted by an assassin; and Arthur served out the remainder of the term.

Nitwitticisms # 2

"DEWEY DEFEATS TRUMAN"

~ *Headline of the Chicago Daily Tribune* on election day 1948. Due to an impending printers' strike, the paper published an early edition, before the polls had closed. Political pundits were predicting that New York Governor Thomas Dewey would easily oust Truman from the White House, so the Trib went with that story. However, Truman trounced Dewey, and famously posed for news photos, holding up a copy of the issue with the embarrassingly wrong headline.

"We pray for MacArthur's erection."

~ *Signs and banners* displayed by Japanese citizens, when Gen. Douglas MacArthur was considering running for U.S. President

"Oh, goddammit! We forgot the silent prayer."

~ *U.S. President Dwight D. Eisenhower, after a cabinet meeting*

"If we don't succeed, we run the risk of failure."

~ *U.S. President George W. Bush*

"Bruce Sutter has been around for a while and he's pretty old. He's 35 years old. That will give you some idea of how old he is."

~ *Sportscaster Ron Fairy*

"To be blunt, people would vote for me. They just would. Maybe because I'm so good looking. I don't know."

~ Donald Trump, billionaire real estate owner, considering a run for the U.S. presidency

"Yes, I would defend Adolf Hitler. And I would win."

~ Alan Dershowitz, Harvard University law professor and high-profile defense attorney

Natural Selection at Work

Watching

5h	A woman shopping at an Idaho Walmart was killed when her 2-year-old son reached into her purse and **shot her with her own handgun.** The New York Times

Do you think the human species might be evolutionarily self-correcting?

"Historians record the names of royal bastards,
but cannot tell us the origin of wheat."

~ Jean Henri Fabré, French scientist, philosopher

On a Clear Day . . .

How far can the eye see?

Well, if you're standing on level ground – which means the Earth's curvature is the only thing limiting the range of your vision – and you're between 5 feet and 6 feet tall, the horizon will be about 3 miles away.

Further than that, everything at ground level drops out of sight due to the curvature.

By the way, people in Columbus' day did not typically believe the Earth was flat. Astronomers had known it was spherical for several centuries, and had even estimated its diameter fairly accurately.

PBI # 8: Thirty Lies Per Second

Next time you're watching a TV documentary about people doing something dangerous or arduous – climbing up a mountain face, slashing their way through a jungle, or opening an ancient tomb – step out of the TV-induced trance for a moment, back up, and ask yourself "Who's filming this?"

How did the camera operator get to the top of the mountain before the climbers got there, in order to film them from above, making that last heroic ascent? Could that be a re-enactment?

Then consider that there's not only a camera operator, but also a sound technician with a boom mike, a couple of "gofers", a producer, and probably a retinue of people cooking their meals and driving them around.

If you saw all of that – a wide-angle shot they never show – the danger, drama, and spontaneity might seem less compelling. TV, as they say, is "thirty lies per second."

Uncle Bud Must Be a Good Guy, Huh?

While driving through the countryside in the American northwest, I spotted a large billboard, announcing,

Uncle Bud's Used Cars

"Well," I thought, "that's comforting. 'Uncle Bud' – with a name like that, he'd just have to be as honest as the day is long. A guy named Uncle Bud wouldn't cheat you, would he?"

Then I thought, "Damned right he would. That's probably why he goes by that business name – to set you up for the swindle."

Well, maybe that's a bit too harsh?

Or, maybe not . . .

"I am free of all prejudice. I hate everyone equally."

~ *W.C. Fields, American comic actor*

Randy Rabbits

Scientists report that male rabbits, when stressed or threatened, can retract their testicles all the way inside their abdomens.

The significance of this fact is not clear.

Is Your "Bucket" Leaking?

Each of us has a psychological "bucket."

It's our inner reservoir of positive energy that enables us to engage other people with good will, kindness, consideration, generosity, care and concern, acceptance, and respect.

And all of our buckets are leaky, to some extent or other.

At those times when our buckets are pretty well topped up, and not leaking very much, we feel good about ourselves and we're likely to act in ways other people experience as "nourishing" – we help them feel good about themselves.

And when our internal buckets get leaky, we're more inclined to treat others in ways they experience as "toxic" – we say and do things that cause them to feel offended, insulted, ignored, devalued, disrespected, unappreciated, or unloved.

Most of us manage to keep our buckets fairly well topped up, most of the time. Some days we're more "up" than others, but over the long run most of us realize the value of expressing this positive energy to those around us.

And then there are some people whose buckets are chronically low and leaky.

You can easily detect leaking psychological buckets in operation when people (including you) say or do unkind things. The person who likes to "needle" others; the one who always has to be right; the one who's the chronic debater; the one who's always showing how smart he is and how dumb everybody else is; the one who boisterously calls attention to herself; the one who's just rude and insensitive – all have leaky buckets.

When their self-esteem and self-confidence start to sag, their internal buckets start to leak, and they run low on the energy of loving kindness. They feel the need to "do a number" on somebody. The result: toxic behavior and alienation from others.

68

Check Your Bucket for Leaks

You can conclude that your internal bucket is leaking or getting low at a particular moment if:

- ✓ You're moody, short-tempered, and don't feel friendly.
- ✓ You "fly off the handle" at small provocations.
- ✓ You start an argument with somebody over something they've said, and you refuse to call a truce until you've defeated them – to your satisfaction.
- ✓ You feel the impulse to "fix" somebody – giving them unsought advice; preaching to them; showing them they're wrong; or making fun of them.
- ✓ You "kick the cat" – or a person – who happens to come along when you're angry or irritated about something they had no part of.
- ✓ You lose touch with your sense of humor – things don't seem funny any more.

Think about the toxic behaviors you've seen in others – and in yourself – and add your own symptoms to this short list.

How Do You Fix a Leaky Bucket?

The fix for a leaky bucket is just to put yourself into a better mood. Find that generous, caring person in yourself again, and let him or her take over. Part of the emotional recharge is mental – changing your "attitude" in a few seconds, and part of it is actually physical.

For example, you can change your mood by changing your posture. Stand up, look up, stretch your arms overhead, take in a few deep breaths, and remind yourself how lucky you are to be alive. Move around, exercise your muscles, take a few more deep breaths, and "become a better person."

Then, bring up the "attitude of gratitude." Find the memory of that special feeling state you're in when you're OK with the world. You're grateful for all that you have in life, and you want the best of everything for others as well. Let that feeling fill up your body – or your bucket – and you'll find it much easier to give positive energy to others.

And, as you and I well know, what you give is what you get back.

Robin Hood on Wheels

Activists in the town of Keene, New Hampshire have declared war on their government, claiming that parking fines are excessive and offensive to the citizens.

They go around putting coins into expired parking meters, to save their fellow citizens from the stiff fines they would otherwise have to pay.

They refer to themselves as modern-day "Robin Hood" activists, interfering with the collection of "the king's tariffs."

They claim to have saved over 8,000 drivers from the onerous fines.

Come On In – Or, Don't

Sign on the door of a coffee shop in San Francisco:

> Push.
> If that doesn't work,
> pull.
> If that doesn't work,
> We're closed.

"I always know when I've encountered a really great idea, because of the feeling of terror it causes in me."

~ *James Franck, German physicist, Nobel Laureate*

They Start 'Em Young in Peru

The youngest mother in history, according to reputable medical experts, was five years, seven months and 21 days old at the time she gave birth. Lina Medina, a Peruvian girl from the Andean village of Ticrapo, gave birth to a boy via caesarean section in May 1939.

Her parents initially thought their daughter had a large abdominal tumor, but astonished physicians confirmed that she was pregnant. They estimated that she had been menstruating for several years and had fully developed ovaries. Authorities suspected her father of incest, but had no convincing evidence.

Prominent physicians from the U.S. and other countries traveled to her village, examined her, and documented her case extensively.

Science Class Isn't Working

It appears that more Americans prefer to believe in creationism, angels, and UFOs than in global warming and evolution.

A survey commissioned by the *National Geographic Channel*, in connection with its new TV series "Chasing UFOs," found that 36 percent of Americans believe UFOs are extra-terrestrial vehicles. One in 10 respondents said they had personally witnessed an alien spaceship.

> *'79 percent of people think the government has kept information about UFOs a secret from the public.'*
>
> *- NatGeo survey*

Surveys by other reputable researchers like the Gallup organization, Smithsonian, and others find that:

- ❖ 55 percent of Americans say they believe in angels.
- ❖ Only 39 percent say they accept the concept of evolution.
- ❖ Only 36 percent say they believe global warning is partly anthropogenic (i.e. caused by human activity).
- ❖ 34 percent say they believe in ghosts.
- ❖ 34 percent believe in UFOs.

Delving a bit deeper, the research shows that:

As many as 69% of Americans who regularly attend religious services accept the "creationist" viewpoint, i.e. the belief that a single, omnipotent God literally created all there is.

71

This belief tends to be more prevalent among the elderly (the most religious age group), and those with a high school education or less. Among college educated people, and those who attend services less frequently, the percentage falls to about 23 percent.

The average across all populations is about 42 percent in favor of the literal creationist belief system.

Clearly, America is still a prescientific society. For all the popular news about "technology," the gee-whiz pictures from outer space, and the daily breakthroughs in medical research, a large majority of Americans seem to have understood or retained very little from their high school science classes. And their view of scientific questions remains heavily contaminated by religious beliefs handed down over centuries.

According to the U.S. government's National Institute of Science:

> "Surveys conducted in the United States and Europe reveal that many citizens do not have a firm grasp of basic scientific facts and concepts, nor do they have an understanding of the scientific process. In addition, belief in pseudoscience (an indicator of scientific illiteracy) seems to be widespread among Americans and Europeans. Studies also suggest that not many Americans are technologically literate."

What's more distressing, of course, is the number of political candidates, public office holders, and even school board members who show an appalling lack of scientific literacy, and in some cases even anti-scientific biases.

Novelist H.G. Wells observed, "Civilization is more and more a race between education and catastrophe."

Reference: http://www.nsf.gov/statistics/seind04/c7/c7s2.htm

"Me and a book is a party.
Me and a book and a cup of coffee is an orgy."
~ *Robert Fripp, British guitarist, musical composer*

Suicide is Painless – Sometimes

How do the handlers of those suicide bombers keep them motivated, and not afraid to die?

The techniques are many, and they work pretty well. One of them is explaining to the prospective bomber that he'll feel absolutely no pain or discomfort at the instant of the explosion.

The rationale is that the detonation takes a very small amount of time – typically a few thousandths of a second. And, by the time the nerve signals would have traveled to the brain, carrying the message that serious bodily injury has occurred, the brain would no longer exist. It would have been vaporized.

That's a big advantage over other methods of suicide, like shooting it out with the police, getting beaten to death by an angry mob, or setting yourself on fire (that one never did get really popular).

Sounds like a bizarre sales proposition, but – hey, we're dealing with desperate people in a desperate situation.

PBI # 9: The Psychology of Risk

Human beings are notoriously incapable of realistically estimating risk in situations that arouse emotions like fear or greed (e.g. terrorism or the stock market).

Immediately after the 9-11 bombing, millions of Americans swore they would never fly on airplanes again. With 6,000-plus flights over the continental U.S. every day, one's chances of riding on a hijacked airliner – even if a hijacking occurred every single day – would be about 1 in 6,000.

That's roughly the same as one's chances of getting run down by an elephant. Yet thousands of people would drive their cars to Las Vegas or Atlantic City, hoping to beat the odds against the casinos – while cleverly cheating death at the hands of hijackers.

Suicide Tourism?

There seems to be a thriving market for "medical tourism," which involves people traveling to developing countries to get facelifts and other elective surgeries much more cheaply than in their home countries. "See Thailand and get your facelift while you're here," the marketing message goes.

Now comes "suicide tourism."

According to an article in *The Week* magazine:

> "In Europe, "going to Switzerland" has become a euphemism for assisted suicide. As many as 200 people a year are traveling to the country for the sole purpose of ending their lives.

> "[. . .] as many as six independent companies operate in and around Zurich, providing their mostly foreign customers with access to medically assisted suicide. A recent BBC investigation found that many [. . .] customers were able to travel to Switzerland, see a doctor, and die – all in one day."

This sounds like the rise of a new cottage industry. A number of questions come up about the service:

- ✓ Do you only have to buy a one-way air ticket?
- ✓ What do they do with your remains – ship you home; cremate you; bury you in the Alps?
- ✓ Do they offer funerals? Might your relatives come to your funeral and make a vacation out of it?
- ✓ If they bury you there, wouldn't you need to become a citizen; or at least get a long-term visa?

Just asking . . .

Medical trips are sometimes referred to as "surgical vacations." But, doesn't the idea of a "suicide vacation" sound a bit strange?

"Faced with the choice between changing one's mind
and proving there is no need to do so,
almost everyone gets busy on the proof."
~ *John Kenneth Galbraith, British economist*

Smart-Assed Flight Attendants

All too rarely, airline attendants make an effort to make the in-flight safety lecture and their other announcements a bit more entertaining. Here are some real examples that have been heard or reported:

On a Continental Flight with a very senior flight attendant crew, the pilot said,

> "Ladies and gentlemen, we've reached cruising altitude and will be turning down the cabin lights. This is for your comfort and to enhance the appearance of your flight attendants."

Other smart-alecky lines reported:

> "Please be sure to take all your belongings. If you're going to leave anything, please make sure it's something we can sell."

> "There may be 50 ways to leave your lover, but there are only 4 ways out of this airplane."

> "Thank you for flying Delta Business Express. We hope you enjoyed giving us the business as much as we enjoyed taking you for a ride."

> "Please take care when opening the overhead compartments because, after a landing like that, sure as hell everything has shifted."

> "Welcome aboard Southwest Flight XXX to YYY. To operate your seat belt, insert the metal tab into the buckle, and pull tight. It works just like every other seat belt, and if you don't know how to operate one, you probably shouldn't be out in public unsupervised."

> "In the event of a sudden loss of cabin pressure, masks will descend from the ceiling. Stop screaming, grab the mask, and put it over your face. If you have a small child traveling with you, secure your mask before assisting with theirs. If you are traveling with more than one small child . . . pick your favorite."

> "Weather at our destination is 50 degrees with some broken clouds, but we'll try to have them fixed before we arrive."

> "Thank you, and remember – nobody loves you, or your money, more than Southwest Airlines."

"Your seat cushions can be used for flotation, and in the event of an emergency water landing, please paddle to shore and take them with our compliments."

"We ask you to please remain seated as Captain Kangaroo bounces us to the terminal."

From the pilot during his welcome message:

"Delta airlines is pleased to have some of the best flight attendants in the industry. Unfortunately, none of them are on this flight."

After an exceptionally hard landing, an elderly woman asked the pilot, who was standing at the exit door,

"Did we land – or were we shot down?"

Technology Makes Our Lives More Interesting

Apple announced today that it has developed a breast implant that can store and play music.

The iTit will cost from $99 to $499, depending on cup and speaker size.

This is considered a major social breakthrough, because women are always complaining about men staring at their breasts and not listening to them.

I don't make this stuff up – I just pass it on . . .

Your Emotional Reset Button

How long does it take you to calm down and get your emotions back to normal after someone or something upsets you?

Someone insults you, or cuts you off in traffic, or says or does something inconsiderate. Maybe you get angry, or frustrated, or offended.

How long do you stay in this "afterburn" mode?

Does it seem strange to suggest that you have a choice? "Oh, no," some will say. "I can't suppress my feelings – I just react."

Well, strangely, you can indeed change your emotional state fairly easily. All you have to do is press your emotional reset button.

You didn't know you have an emotional reset button? Sure you do. It's located on your forehead, just above and between your eyebrows.

After every emotional provocation, there's a phase where you become vaguely aware that you've wigged out, and you start to "come down."

As soon as you get to that point, tell yourself, "I've been angry – or hurt, or offended, or indignant, or insulted, or whatever – long enough now. It's time to get back to normal."

Then, just touch the tip of your index finger to that imaginary place on your forehead, and pretend you're pushing a reset button.

Instantly, your attention will switch to that place and that sensation, and – because your brain can only pay attention to one thing at a time – the emotional provocation gets pushed out of your mind. After a few seconds, you'll be much closer to "normal."

If something has really pissed you off, just push the button again, every minute or two, and focus your attention closely on the sensation of touching your forehead.

Try it – it works.

"There is nothing more frightening than ignorance in action."

~ Johann Wolfgang von Goethe, German philosopher

The Fat Comes Back

Have you noticed that when one of your friends is on a diet, and losing lots of weight, he's just full of good advice about what you should do to lose weight, too?

"What did you have for breakfast?" he'll ask.

"Oatmeal."

"Did you put milk on it?"

"Yeah."

"Skim milk?"

"No, regular milk."

"Well, see – that's where you made your mistake. Whole milk has too many calories. You should use skim milk."

"Oh, I see," you nod.

"Do you put dressing on your salad?"

"Why do you ask?"

"Because salad dressing has a lot of hidden calories. They put sugar in it."

"Oh, thanks for letting me know that."

You have to listen to this holier-than-thou crap for a few weeks, or a month, or maybe even a couple of months. Then – *it stops*.

About six months later, you noticed he's gained it all back.

Tell the truth: don't you feel just a little bit of vengeful glee when you see that he's just as fat as he was?

Favorite Lame Joke # 4

Bubba was showing off his new motorcycle around the gas station, and he offered one of the local gals a ride.

As it was a chilly day, he gave her his extra jacket to wear. "Put it on backwards," he advised, so the cold wind won't get at you."

She slipped her arms into the opposite sides of the jacket, he zipped it up the back, and off they went.

He got a bit too rambunctious with his cornering and maneuvering over the narrow country roads, and after a particularly violent bump, he looked around and discovered she wasn't there.

"Omigod!" he lamented. "I hope she's all right!"

He turned the cycle around and roared back over the route. Topping a hill, he could see a small crowd of farmers standing in the middle of the road, surrounding the young lady, who was sitting there motionless.

He skidded to a halt, jumped off the bike, and ran up to the group.

"Is she OK?" he pleaded.

"Well sir," one of the farmers said, removing his John Deere ball cap and scratching his head, "she was all right when we got here, but since we turned her head around the right way, she hasn't spoke."

The Official Sport of Maryland is . . .

The official sport of the State of Maryland is – are you ready for this? – *jousting*. Maryland was the first U.S. state to adopt an official sport, in 1962. According to the state's official website:

> Jousting tournaments have been held in Maryland since early colonial times but became increasingly popular after the Civil War. Retaining the pageantry and customs of medieval tournaments, modern competitors are called "knights" or "maids", and many dress in colorful costumes. Men, women and children compete equally with skill and horsemanship determining the class.

> Tournaments conducted in Maryland are "ring tournaments" which involve charging a horse at full-gallop through an 80-yard course toward suspended rings. Using a long, fine-tipped lance, the rider has 8 seconds to complete the course and "spear" the rings, scoring points accordingly. From three equally-spaced arches, rings are hung 6 feet 9 inches above the ground and range in diameter from one-quarter inch to nearly two inches depending upon the skill level of the contestant. A family sport, jousting skills frequently are passed from one generation to the next.

> Today, jousting competitions are held from May through October in Maryland.

"A human being should be able to change a diaper,
plan an invasion, butcher a hog, conn a ship,
design a building, write a sonnet, balance accounts,
build a wall, set a bone, comfort the dying,
take orders, give orders, cooperate, act alone,
solve equations, analyze a new problem,
program a computer, cook a tasty meal,

fight efficiently, die gallantly.

Specialization is for insects."

~ Robert Heinlein, American science fiction writer

PBI # 10: A Picture is Worth . . .

One of our traditional slogans is "a picture is worth a thousand words." Possibly so, but the situation you're in might have a big effect on the trade-off. If you're drowning, then shouting one word – "HELP!" – might be worth more than a thousand pictures.

The Wisdom of Yogi

Lawrence Peter ("Yogi") Berra was one of baseball's most accomplished and durable players, as well as a popular and colorful figure. He was known for his linguistically skewed aphorisms.

- o "In theory, there's no difference between theory and practice. But, in practice, there is."

- o "If the people don't want to come out to the ballpark, how ya gonna stop 'em?"

- o "Ninety percent of the game of baseball is half mental."

- o "Always go to other people's funerals, otherwise they won't come to yours."

- o "You can observe a lot just by watching."

- o "He hits from both sides of the plate. He's amphibious."

- o "It's like déja vu all over again."

- o "It ain't over till it's over."

When his wife asked where he wanted to be buried, he said, "Surprise me."

Gays in the Military? Not a New Issue

Lest we conclude that homosexuality amongst soldiers interferes with their units' capacity to fight, consider the case of the Sacred

Band of Thebes, a hundred-percent gay fighting force that became famous in Alexander's time, around 325 BC.

Numbering about 300–400, they were permanently partnered, and partners fought side by side in many engagements.

According to historical reports, they were athletic, fit, strong, skilled at hand-to-hand fighting, and exceedingly ferocious. They typically fought to the death – either you killed them, or they killed you.

Alexander, and many other Greek generals, typically had teen-aged boys as companions, taking them on long military campaigns. Many Roman generals continued this practice.

In fact, Alexander came to power when his father, Philip of Macedon, died of stab wounds inflicted by his own jealous young lover.

It was not uncommon for soldiers to form close homosexual partnerships with their peers. Greek culture treated these relationships as deeply personal and emotional, on a par with male-female romantic relationships of today.

"When people are free to do as they please,

they usually imitate one another."

~ *Eric Hoffer, American author, essayist*

The Eureka Moment

The French physician and scientist Louis Pasteur advised, "Chance favors the prepared mind."

Some of the most powerful ideas in the history of science came to their inventors while they were daydreaming.

The so-called "eureka" moment, or the "aha" experience, is the culmination of a pre-conscious process known as *incubation*.

Incubation is a stage in which the thinker has temporarily set aside his or her attempts to solve a problem, and has turned to other thoughts. But behind the curtain of consciousness, the brain's many computers are always at work.

Most of us have had the eureka experience from time to time – that flash of insight that suddenly explains something, or shows us how to solve a problem.

The most notorious example of *Isaac Newton* and the apple, which might or might not have actually occurred, illustrates the process. According to legend, Newton had left London and the university to stay at his parents' farm in the English countryside. While sitting under a tree on a pleasant day, he suddenly conceived of the phenomenon of gravity, as a powerful force of nature. Legend has it that he saw an apple fall from a tree, and became fascinated with the simple idea that everything fell toward the earth. From there, he worked out the concept of gravity as one of the fundamental forces of nature.

Galileo, who left the planet in the same year that Newton arrived, had a similar daydreaming insight. While sitting quietly in a church, he absently watched a candle fixture suspended from the ceiling, as it swung slowly back and forth in the slight breeze. The length of the swing increased and increased with the breeze, but he had a sudden realization: the period of the pendulum he was watching – the length of time needed to complete one full swing from end to end and back – seemed to stay the same. On the longer swings, the candle moved faster, but the total swing time was constant. This led him to experiments that verified that the period of a pendulum depended on only one variable: the length of the chain or string holding it up. The weight of the object made no difference.

In 1816, the French physician *René Laennec* got the idea for the stethoscope while watching boys at play. He was perplexed because he couldn't easily hear the heart sounds of one of his patients, an obese woman, by the usual method of putting his ear to her chest. The boys were playing with a length of pipe; one would whisper into the end of the pipe and the other would try to hear it from the other end. Laennec suddenly visualized a similar device for listening to the internal sounds of the patient. He quickly devised a number of variations on the design, and evolved what became the modern stethoscope.

And in 1865, the Austrian scientist *Friedrich August Kekulé von Stradonitz* reportedly figured out the structure of the *benzene* molecule, while dozing beside his fireplace. In his half-dream state, he saw a vivid image of a snake biting its own tail. He realized that the molecule would have to be arranged as a closed hexagon, with carbon atoms at each of the six points.

The next time you're stuck on a problem or decision, you might try incubating it. Dwell on it for a while, and then turn your attention to other things. Maybe a good idea will come to you when you least expect it.

Try This Quick Quiz

If you're one of those smart people who know lots of stuff, search your mental database for these questions; then check the answers below.

1. How long did the Hundred Years' War last?
2. Which country makes Panama hats?
3. From which animal do we get catgut?
4. In which month do Russians celebrate the October Revolution?
5. What is a camel's hair brush made of?
6. The Canary Islands in the Pacific are named after what animal?
7. What was King George VI's first name?
8. What color is a purple finch?
9. Where do Chinese gooseberries come from?
10. What's the color of the "black box" in a commercial airplane?

Answers:

1. 116 years
2. Ecuador
3. Sheep and horses
4. November
5. Squirrel fur
6. Dogs
7. Albert

8. Crimson

9. New Zealand

10. Orange – for visibility

"It is a capital mistake to theorise in advance of the facts."
~ *Sherlock Holmes, mythical British detective*

Why Teachers Get Gray Early

One of those charming stories that circulate in the public education community concerns an essay exam assigned by an American fifth-grade teacher. The essay question asked the students to name as many parts of the human body as they could think of, and tell what they do. One child wrote:

"The human body consists of the Brainium,

the Borax, and the Abominable Cavity.

The Brainium contains the brain.

The Borax contains the lungs, the liver, and other living things.

The Abominable Cavity contains the bowels,

of which there are five – a, e, i, o, and u."

This is the kind of experience that causes some teachers to retire early, and others to wonder whether the whole process of education makes sense.

This Will Diagnose Your Age

Have you ever seen "Burma-Shave" signs in the American countryside? If so, you're definitely in the older population. If not, you might have heard of them.

The Burma-Shave company, founded in 1925, started advertising their shaving cream by planting signs along the sides of country roads in America. Each set of five signs offered a rhyming bit of wisdom, usually humorous, with another sign touting the name of the product.

Some examples:

HARDLY A DRIVER
IS NOW ALIVE
WHO PASSED
ON HILLS
AT 75
BURMA-SHAVE

PAST
SCHOOLHOUSES
TAKE IT SLOW
LET THE LITTLE
SHAVERS GROW
BURMA-SHAVE

IF YOU DISLIKE
BIG TRAFFIC FINES
SLOW IT DOWN
TILL YOU
CAN READ THESE SIGNS
BURMA-SHAVE

If you enjoy Americana and cultural nostalgia, it's worth a visit to:

burma-shave.org

"No one with a weak stomach
should watch sausage or the law being made."
~ *Oliver Wendell Holmes, U.S. Chief Justice*

We're Watching You

The Wall Street Journal reports that the FBI has files on nearly 80 million Americans, and adds more than 10,000 new ones per day.

Many of the new names come from arrests for minor infractions, and some are connected to "zero tolerance" policies at public schools.

Factoids # 3

- ❖ "Stewardesses" might the longest word one can type with only the left hand. You get a prize if you discover a longer one.

- ❖ "Uncopyrightable" might be the only 15 letter word one can write without repeating a letter. You get a round of applause if you find another one.

- ❖ "Dreamt" might the only English word that ends in the letters "mt." Let me know if you find another one.

- ❖ "Screeched" might be the longest one-syllable word in the English language. You're guaranteed fame and adulation if you find a longer one.

- ❖ The first popular novel ever written on a typewriter: *Tom Sawyer*, by Mark Twain.

- ❖ The sentence "The quick brown fox jumps over the lazy dog." uses every letter in the alphabet. That's one reason typing teachers used to make their students type it as an exercise.

- ❖ The U.S. Declaration of Independence was not signed on July 4th. That was just the date when the Continental Congress finally approved it. Only two delegates signed it on that day, John Hancock and Charles Thomson. Most of the rest signed on August 2, but the last signature didn't go on until 5 years later. Two of the delegates, John Dickinson and Robert R. Livingston, never signed it.

PBI # 11: Smarter Kids, or Dumber Ones?

We're being sold the idea, these days, that our kids are smarter than we are.

The evidence offered for this is that they "multi-task." When your teen-ager has the TV on while listening to her MP3 player, talking with her friend on the cell phone, updating her social-network Web page, surfing the Internet on her laptop, and spilling cookie crumbs on her algebra book, she's said to be multi-tasking. And that's taken as a sign of some kind of high competence. "Tech-savvy," she is.

Bad news: the human brain is incapable of multi-tasking. She's not multi-tasking – she's just "time-slicing," which means that her attention hops around from one task to another, but she can only attend to one thing at a time. Each of the "n" tasks gets only one-nth of the attention – minus an "overhead" deduction for the time spent switching and re-orienting.

Here's a simple test to prove that you and your kids can only do one thing at a time with your conscious minds. Lift your right foot from the floor and begin moving it clockwise, in a circling motion. After about five seconds, while you continue moving it like that, start moving your right hand in a counter-clockwise circling movement. Can't do it, can you? Whichever action you concentrate on forces your brain to run all other actions on "autopilot."

Multi-tasking, in its highly praised form as seen in teen-agers, may actually be a pathological inability to concentrate on one thing for any significant length of time. By the time we fully understand this phenomenon, we may have a whole generation of adults who have the attention span of a gnat.

And the tech-savvy part? Note that all of the consumer electronic gadgets that are so popular today have been dumbed down by the technological wizards to the point where they can be operated by a monkey. Very few kids could explain how a cell phone is made or how it works. Ditto for the PC, the iPod, iPad, iPhone, smart phones, and the Internet. They're enthusiastic consumers of electronic gadgets. But tech-savvy? Unfortunately, no. That's one reason the U.S. is steadily losing its lead in almost all aspects of science and technology.

So, are our kids really smarter than we are? Let's hope so, but . . .

Cleanse Your Mind With a "Media Fast"

Mohandas Gandhi, one of the most revered thinkers and thought leaders in history, made a habit of spending one day each week in silence. Usually on a Monday, he wouldn't speak, nor would he be spoken to. He used the time for reflection, reading, and listening to his own mind. Through silent work, meditation, and exercise, he attempted to rediscover the center of his intelligence. Many of us could benefit from finding the wisdom of our own silence.

While many of us may think that such a practice would be completely impossible in today's sensory-overload world, consider that in his later years Gandhi often met with political organizers, journalists, and high government officials, as well as the students at his *ashram*. His attention was in great demand, yet he found time to meditate, spin cotton thread on his primitive spinning wheel, and study the classics of religious literature. If Gandhi could do it, so can we – if we think it's important enough. The challenges are different for us, but no greater than those Gandhi faced.

Admittedly, so much conspires against our mental peace, tranquility, and privacy. Almost everywhere we go in the modern media-soaked culture, sights and sounds demand our attention. The radio in the car; the boom-box blaring in the hands of teen-agers walking by, or from another teen's car; the television in the airport waiting area and the relentless security announcements over the public address system; the in-flight movie or the video news on the airplane; the rock music playing over the sound system in the coffee shop; the continuous sports footage in the bar or restaurant; the person talking on the cell phone at the next table; the jarring sights and sounds of TV news; the raucous diatribes of political talk shows on radio; and of course the relentless hammering of the TV set at home.

You can reduce the cultural noise level coming into your mind in stages. Consider making one day per week a TV-free day. (This is a movement that is gaining acceptance in the U.S. and other media-based cultures.) Leave the TV set turned off from midnight to midnight. You may need to negotiate with your family – or use your personal authority – to get them to cooperate. Simply staying out of the room while a TV is operating doesn't help much to free your mind if you can still hear it.

Once you can get through a full TV-free day on a regular basis, start locking other media channels out of your consciousness. Don't watch recorded video material and don't go to the movies on your media-free day.

Progress from there to leaving all radios turned off on your media-free day. That includes drive-time radio broadcasts and especially radio news. Leave the music turned off as you drive. Make a conscious effort to choose your activities so that you'll seldom be exposed to other people's media pollution.

Once you've become comfortable with turning off all broadcast and televisual media, progress to leaving newspapers and magazines out of your life on your media-free day. Don't even read the advertising material that comes in your mail on that day.

So: no TV, no movies, no videotaped or digital video watching, no radio, no music, no newspapers, and no magazines. For your next challenge, stay off of the Internet for the full 24 hours of your media-free day. Once you can do that, make it through the day with your cell phone switched off.

The first few times you experience a full-day media fast, you may feel rather strange, possibly somewhat disoriented, maybe even deprived. You'll start to become conscious of how much of your time and attention are confiscated by the passive consumption of cultural junk food.

You may feel a sense of something missing – a familiar ritual that's been taken away. Your sense of time may seem less compartmentalized and less incremental.

Eventually, you'll probably experience a general sense of greater calm, a less frenetic sense of what's going on around you, and relief from a lingering, low-grade sense of urgency. You'll have no choice but to listen to your own interior monologue. Without the many distractions imposed upon your consciousness, you may enjoy spending more time with your thoughts. Ask yourself "What am I learning as I clear my mind of media pollution, and how can this special state of attention help me?"

After I removed all broadcast TV signals from my home, over ten years ago, I experienced a noticeable shift in my state of mind. I felt more placid, more optimistic, more open to new experience, and more charitable toward myself and others. It's no exaggeration to say that I felt that my mind had been "cleansed," to some extent. I still watch lots of educational lectures, documentaries, and selected movies from time to time – particularly the old classics, musicals, and comedies. I feel no loss in not having broadcast video material in my personal environment.

What Do America's Leaders Read?

The Wall Street Journal is read by the people who run the country.

The Washington Post is read by people who think they run the country.

The New York Times is read by people who think they should run the country and who are very good at crossword puzzles.

The Boston Globe is read by people whose parents used to run the country and did a much better job of it.

USA Today is read by people who think they should run the country, but don't really understand *The New York Times*. They do, however, like the statistics shown in those cute little pie charts.

The New York Daily News is read by people who aren't too sure who's running the country and don't really care, so long as they can get a seat on the train.

The New York Post is read by people who don't care who's running the country, so long as they're doing something really scandalous, preferably while intoxicated.

The Los Angeles Times is read by people who wouldn't mind running the country – if they could find the time – and if they didn't have to leave Southern California to do it.

The San Francisco Chronicle is read by people who aren't sure it's actually a country, or that anyone should actually be running it, but certainly not Republicans.

The National Enquirer is read by people trapped in line at grocery stores.

"And how am I to face the odds
of man's bedevilment, and God's?
I, a stranger and afraid
in a world I never made."
~ *A.E. Housman, British scholar and poet; from "Last Poems"*

Maybe We Get the Politicians We Deserve

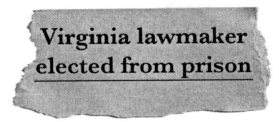

Maybe we get the elected officials we deserve – maybe even the ones we want.

Joseph Morrissey, who had resigned his seat in the Virginia state legislature after a scandal involving sex with an underage girl, changed his party affiliation from Democrat to independent, and ran for office again. This time, he campaigned from his jail cell.

He won 43 percent of the votes, easily beating candidates from both of the major parties.

Party leaders tried to prevent him from taking office, but did not succeed.

He won't be able to participate in any late-night legislative sessions, considering that jail rules require him to be back in his cell by 7:30 pm.

He'll be back in the office soon, though. The court reduced his 12-month sentence to 6 months, with a work-release provision that allowed him to practice law and run for office.

You gotta give him his propers – he's got what my Jewish friends call *(c)hutzpah*.

What's the Name of That Thingy . . .

That groove on your face, that runs from just under your nose to the top of your upper lip?

That anatomical feature is called the *philtrum*.

Now, try to work that into a conversation.

Sell 'em Shovels – Or Jeans

Mark Twain advised,

> "When everybody is out digging for gold, the business to be in is selling shovels."

During the famous California gold rush in the 1850s, lots of prospectors bought shovels, but very few of them struck it rich. In fact, most of them lost their shirts – and shovels.

But the guy who made a bundle was Levi Strauss, a Bavarian immigrant who came to San Francisco and began selling them heavy work pants made of canvas.

He opened a factory, improved the product by changing to a special heavy-duty denim material he brought from France, called "genes," which came to be known popularly as "jeans."

He also added copper rivets at key stress points like pockets and the front opening.

Strauss's blue jeans wear well – they've become an iconic American product and brand, still selling strongly to this day.

Strauss used his profits from selling blue jeans to launch other businesses and investments, and soon became a very wealthy man.

Ironically, the aspiring gold miners who were going broke were the ones who made him wealthy.

Maybe Twain had a good point – but it isn't only about shovels.

"There is one thing stronger than all the armies of the world: and that is an idea whose time has come."

~ *Victor Hugo, French novelist*

Where Have All the Soldiers Gone?

Stars and Stripes magazine, the semi-official voice of the military community, reports that fewer than 30 percent of Americans are qualified for military duty.

The other 70 percent flunk out due to causes like obesity, substance abuse, criminal history, or not completing high school.

✪ ✪ ✪ ✪ ✪

"It is not who is right, but what is right that is important."

~ *Thomas Huxley, British philosopher*

✪ ✪ ✪ ✪ ✪

Why Do Some Coins Have Ridges?

A U.S. dime has 118 ridges, or "reeds" around the edge. A U.S. quarter has 119.

The Coinage Act of 1792, which created the U.S. Mint, directed that $10, $5 and $2.50 coins (known as eagles, half-eagles, and quarter-eagles) be made of their – current – face value in gold; and dollar, half-dollar, quarter-dollar, dime, and half-dime coins were to be made of their value in silver.

Immediately, crooks began shaving the outer rims off the coins and collecting the shavings to re-sell. The Mint countered by adding the reeded edges to make the shaved coins easy to detect. One-cent and half-cent coins, made of cheaper copper, were not valuable enough to shave or counterfeit.

Coin-shaving had been a common practice in Europe for many years, especially before paper currency arrived. People typically refused to accept shaved coins being offered in trade, and they always tried to spend them first. This led to the hoarding of intact coins, and the circulation of inferior ones.

Thus, Sir Thomas Gresham gave us "Gresham's Law," which declares that,

"Bad money drives good money out of circulation."

PBI # 12: More Government, Less Government?

Many Americans are currently distressed, disappointed, and disgusted with their political leadership in Washington. Destructive deadlock seems to be the order of the day, and probably will remain so for quite some time to come. However, there may be a perverse up-side to all of the un-statesmanlike behavior: *it could be worse.*

Humorist Will Rogers said,

> "You ought to be glad you're not getting all the government you're paying for."

I find the idea of an efficient government to be a rather terrifying thought. Perhaps the founders of the republic set up the system of "checks and balances," knowing the awful consequences that might occur if one of the major houses of government were to come under the control of a skillful political operator – or party – with despotic ambitions.

The political system they designed almost guarantees a slow-moving, bureaucratic, unimaginative process that resists the influence of both talent and ambition. It's a system that's amazingly resilient to human dumbness and human perversity. As much as I'd like to see more intelligent effort and more intelligent solutions, on most days I take a certain comfort in knowing that they're all tied together at the ankles.

Tweets, Twits, and Twats: Are the Media Making You Crazy?

When actor Charlie Sheen, at one time America's favorite over-aged celebrity delinquent, decided to share his manic thoughts with the world, over 1,000,000 people joined his Twitter flock in a few days – a world record at the time.

When Britney Spears climbed out of a limousine in Manhattan, having apparently misplaced her underpants, the view of her primary asset became one of the most often downloaded images in Internet history.

Sports Illustrated, for many years an uninspiring men's magazine, saw declining readership and profits for years. When the editors introduced the "annual swimsuit issue" (swimming is a recognized sport, don't you know), it raked in more profit than the rest of the year's issues combined.

Our Two Diets

Healthcare researchers report that over half of Americans are now significantly overweight, with at least thirty percent of them qualifying as obese. Statisticians are beginning to suggest that life expectancy of coming generations might actually be lower than for their parents.

And media researchers report that Americans now spend as much money – and time – on "mental junk food" as on junk food for their bodies. And the long-term effects on the culture might turn out to be even greater.

Will the Earth Wobble Off Its Axis?

Ninety percent of the Earth's people live in the northern hemisphere. And they're getting fatter.

Check it out on the map: a big percentage of the southern hemisphere is ocean. Considering that Antarctica – virtually uninhabited and uninhabitable – takes up a big part of that, there's not a whole lot of turf left to occupy.

Is the Internet Making Us Obese?

Ordering products online usually saves time, and often saves money. It also saves calories. You hit a few keys, click the mouse, and open your front door to receive the parcel. Calories burned: about 25.

Before the Internet, you had to get in your car, drive to the mall, park, walk to the shop, carry the stuff to your car, drive home – maybe stop for gas – and open the front door for the second time. Calories burned: about 200.

If you average two online purchases per week, you'll avoid burning 17,500 calories over a year. That's equivalent to about five pounds of body fat. If just ten million Americans do this – a very conservative estimate – there will be about 25,000 tons of extra fat accumulating every year in the U.S. alone.

The cure: every time you place an online order, get on your treadmill for twenty minutes.

Writers Talk About Writing

"The difference between the right word and the almost-right word is like the difference between lightning and a lightning bug."

~ Mark Twain, American novelist and humorist

"Substitute 'damn' every time you're inclined to write 'very.' Your editor will delete it and the writing will be just as it should be."

~ Mark Twain

"The writer's life is a dog's life – but the only one worth living."

~ Gustave Flaubert, French novelist

"I'm not a writer with a drinking problem. I'm a drinker with a writing problem."

~ Brendan Behan, Irish novelist

"The road to hell is paved with adverbs."

~ Stephen King, best-selling American mystery writer

"Fiction is the truth inside the lie."

~ Stephen King

"Don't tell me the moon is shining; show me the glint of light on broken glass."

~ Anton Chekhov, Russian novelist

"History will be kind to me, for I intend to write it."

~ Winston S. Churchill, British statesman

"When I think of all the harm the Bible has done, I despair of ever writing anything to equal it."

~ Oscar Wilde, British poet and satirist

"I can shake off everything as I write; my sorrows disappear, my courage is reborn."

~ Anne Frank, Jewish child of the holocaust

"If my doctor told me I had only six minutes to live, I wouldn't brood. I'd type a little faster."
~ *Isaac Asimov, prolific American science fiction writer*

"Everywhere I go I'm asked if I think the university stifles writers. My opinion is that they don't stifle enough of them. There's many a best-seller that could have been prevented by a good teacher."
~ *Flannery O'Connor, Irish novelist*

"Everybody probably does have a book in them, but in most cases that's where it should stay."
~ *Christopher Hitchens, British political commentator*

"Writing a novel is like driving a car at night. You can see only as far as your headlights, but you can make the whole trip that way."
~ *Edgar Lawrence ("E.L.") Doctorow, American novelist*

"I can't imagine a romance novel published today where the hero rapes the heroine and she falls in love with him."
~ *Julia Quinn, American romance novelist*

"If you can't annoy somebody, there is little point in writing."
~ *Kingsley Amis, British novelist*

"Writing is like prostitution. First you do it for love, and then for a few close friends, and then for money."
~ *Moliére (Jean-Baptiste Poquelin), French actor and playwright*

"There are three rules for writing a best-selling novel. Unfortunately, no one knows what they are."
~ *W. Somerset Maugham*

You Never Know What You Might Find at the Flea Market

In 1989, a Philadelphia man found one of the original copies of the U.S. Declaration of Independence, hidden in the back of a picture frame he bought at a flea market for $4.

One of the few surviving copies from the official first printing of the Declaration, known as the Dunlap Broadside, he found it in excellent condition.

It sold in 2000 for $8.1 million.

Favorite Lame Joke # 5

A young woman telephoned her fiancé from her hotel, while on a business trip out of town. After swapping the general news, she wanted to know whether he'd been taking good care of her cat.

"How's Fluffy?" she asked.

"Fluffy?" he said. "She's dead. Croaked, just like that. All nine lives – Pffft!"

She was stunned by the crude, insensitive way he reported the death of her beloved pet.

"How could you say that?!" she demanded. "That's the cruelest thing I've ever heard anyone say!"

"Well," he said. "She kicked the bucket. What else can I tell you? Do you want me to lie and say she's OK?"

"No," said, "but at least you could try to break the news to me carefully, instead of just blurting out something like that."

"What do you mean, 'break the news carefully?' Dead is dead. How else could I tell you?"

"You're hopeless," she sighed. "You could have just hinted that something was wrong at first, maybe not said that she died. Maybe something like 'She's up on the roof, and the fire department guys are trying to get her down.' Then, when I called the next day, you could say that she fell off the roof and died, or something like that."

"But she didn't fall off the roof. A coyote got her."

"Omigod . . ." "I can't believe you. You just don't get it, do you?"

"I guess not."

"Look, never mind. Just forget about it. Let's talk about something else."

"OK. What do you want to talk about?"

"Well, how's my mother?"

... a long pause on his end ...

"Well ... – uh, she's up on the roof, and ..."

Just Good Business ...

Sign on the wall of the Hibernian Bar, Cork City, Ireland:

> **THOSE WHO DRINK TO FORGET - PLEASE PAY IN ADVANCE.**

Mental Jelly Beans # 2

Weird ideas from comedian George Carlin:

- o If you try to fail, and succeed, which have you done?
- o If one synchronized swimmer drowns, do the rest drown, too?
- o If you were cross-eyed and had dyslexia, could you read OK?
- o If you ate pasta and antipasta, would you still be hungry?
- o Should crematoriums give discounts for burn victims?
- o Why is it called tourist season if we can't shoot at them?
- o How come "abbreviated" is such a long word?
- o Why isn't "phonics" spelled the way it sounds?
- o Whose cruel idea was it for the word "lisp" to have a "s" in it?
- o How is it possible to have a civil war? A holy war?
- o How can a soldier be killed by "friendly fire?"
- o Why is bra singular and panties plural?
- o Why is there an expiration date on sour cream?

- Why is the alphabet in that order? Is it because of that song?
- In California there's a hotline for people in denial. So far, no one has called.

Could We Have Said That Better?

What if the great speeches of history were updated – revised into modern teen-speak?

Take Marc Antony's speech to the Romans at Caesar's funeral ("Friends, Romans, Countrymen – lend me your ears!").

Let's see, in teen-speak, that would be:

> "Dudes! Listen up! Like, we're all here to bury Caesar, right? But first, I got some shit to lay on ya!"

. . . I can't go on . . .

Famous Bad Calls # 2

I guess military people dread being considered pessimistic, so they have to sound confident. But, lots of times, they call it wrong.

First, the French said it:

> "We will have victory in fifteen months."
> ~ *Jean de Tassigny, French general, commander of forces occupying Vietnam (a.k.a. Indochina), December 1950*

> "I expect victory after six more months of hard fighting."
> ~ *Henri-Eugene Navarre, French general,* commander of forces occupying Vietnam, January 1954.

> "Ho Chi Minh is about to capitulate; we are going to beat him."
> ~ *George Bidault, French foreign minister,* February 1954

On May 7, 1954, the French garrison at Dien Bien Phu fell, after a siege of 56 days. The French government ceased all operations and withdrew from Vietnam.

Next, the Americans said it:

"We are not about to send American boys nine or ten thousand miles away to do what Asian boys ought to be doing for themselves."

~ U.S. President Lyndon Johnson, campaigning for re-election, October 1964

"The Vietcong are going to collapse within weeks. Not months, but weeks.

~ Walt Rostow, U.S. State Department official, July 1965

"If I'm elected we'll end this war in six months."

~ Richard Nixon, campaigning for the U.S. presidency, 1968

"We're on our way up – the pendulum is beginning to swing."

~ William Westmoreland, U.S. general, Army Chief of Staff, April 1972

On April 29, 1975, U.S. helicopters evacuated the last Americans from Saigon. What was left of the South Vietnamese government surrendered unconditionally to the forces of North Vietnam.

"The greatest discovery of my generation is that human beings,

by changing the inner attitudes of their minds,

can change the outer aspects of their lives . . .

It is too bad that more people will not accept this tremendous discovery and begin living it."

~ William James, pioneer psychologist

Seven Ways to Be in Love

Many people seem to get themselves into unhappy romantic situations in life because they try to force-fit their relationships into the ready-made "templates" they carry around in their heads – often stored away at an unconscious level.

These romantic templates – or relationship models, if you prefer – are scripted scenarios that define the ways they and their partners are supposed to interact, and they include rules of conduct that they seek to impose.

Some relationships crash out because the two participants are carrying around conflicting models of how the "ideal relationship" should work. They may become so preoccupied with enforcing their own preferred models that conflict, tension, and ego-competition push aside romantic attraction and healthy mutuality.

An individual who's emotionally or socially immature might be so hooked on a particular romantic scenario – or model – as to misread, minimize, or disrespect the needs and interests of the partner. Such a person might crash one potential relationship after another because they haven't learned to deal with their own neediness, jealousy, and self-centeredness. "Serial marriers," for example, very typically tend to repeat history.

Over and over, in working with people who are in a state of relational distress, I see seven main versions of these romantic templates coming into play. By understanding which, if any, of these primary templates an individual might be trying to impose, we can sometimes help them look for more mature and creative alternatives.

The Seven Main Romantic Models

1. The Gravity model. This construct seems to involve a sudden and unexpected loss of self-control, and descent into an emotional pit: "She *fell* madly in love with him." The song lyrics say, "When I *fall in love*, it will be forever – or I'll never fall in love." In a restaurant, I overheard a young woman telling her friends why she couldn't end an increasingly toxic relationship. "You can't help who you love," she proclaimed. Success in romance, it seems, depends on whether you "fall" for the right person or the wrong person.

2. The Destiny model. "We're soul mates. We were made for each other." This construct seems to hold that there's a cosmic matching service, and that each of us has already been assigned the perfect mate. All we have to do is be in the right bar on the right evening – or in the supermarket, or the fitness center – and the cosmic matchmaker will get us together. Occasionally a bit of doubt might creep in: "How do I know if he's really the right one?" An ugly divorce can shake one's belief in this particular model.

3. The Camelot model. Also known as the "love conquers all" model. The organizing principle of this construct seems to be, "If we really love each other, everything will be great." Images of princesses, knights in shining armor, castles, and dragons float through the background of the conversation. The somewhat cynical German philosopher Wolfgang Goethe mused, "Love is an ideal thing. Marriage is real. Confusing the real with the ideal never goes unpunished."

4. *The Merger model.* Also known as the "two people become one" model. This construct seems to dictate that the two lovers must become figurative Siamese twins – emotionally, socially, logistically, financially, spiritually – et cetera. Presumably neither party has the right, or the inclination, to engage in any significant life activity that doesn't include the other. Just as with corporate mergers, it often happens that one participant becomes the acquirer and the other the acquired. And, "de-merging" can often be a difficult and stressful experience.

5. *The Real Estate model.* The centerpiece of this construct seems to be The Relationship – with a capital "R." The abstract idea of a relationship takes on a psychological identity as a co-owned asset. "You have to work at it." "You only get out of it what you put into it." "Our relationship is falling apart." The metaphors suggest that it's like maintaining or remodeling your house – there's always something more to be done.

6. *The Doormat model.* This romantic construct has inspired countless novels, movies, popular songs, and country-western laments. The protagonist is typically afflicted with a passive-dependent attachment to a heartless tormenter, who seems to take perverse pleasure in his or her misery. A needy psychological state of low self-worth compels the victim to sacrifice his or her dignity for the promise of an occasional romantic fix. In the song "My Man," expressed plaintively by Billie Holliday, the lament is, "Two or three girls has he that he likes as well as me – but he's my man. He isn't true; he beats me, too. But, when he takes me in his arms . . ." Frank Sinatra made famous the lyrics, "You're nobody 'til somebody loves you – so find yourself somebody to love."

7. *The Hostage model.* Sort of the inverse of the doormat model, the hostage model asserts an exaggerated sense of emotional entitlement. The hallmark of this construct seems to be an aggressive form of possessiveness, jealousy, and control-seeking. "I just want someone who will be totally honest with me," decodes to "I don't want him or her to find enjoyment in any activity that doesn't revolve around me." The old song lyrics go, "See the pyramids along the Nile . . . Just remember, darling, all the while –

103

you belong to me." At the extreme, this construct can become the template for an abusive relationship.

I'm not suggesting that any or all of these models are necessarily pathological – only that they do often give form to pathological patterns in troubled relationships. Indeed, each one has possibilities for thinking creatively about the choices that arise in forming romantic relationships.

But maybe we don't have to choose one particular template and reject the others. Our self-esteem; our capacity for intimacy; our mature care and concern for others; and our willingness to co-venture are ultimately the most important keys to a successful romantic relationship.

People Talk Funny . . .

Overheard on a plane en route to Hawai'i:

"Nobody goes to Waikiki Beach any more. It's too crowded."

PBI # 13: Who Owns Our Politicians?

Voters and taxpayers often lament that their elected officials have sold out to special interest groups, who expect political favors in return for their campaign contributions. Usually, the politicians and their contributors avoid publicizing their relationships, so it's very difficult to know who's sponsoring a particular office holder.

While it might not be easy to prevent political officials from selling their services, there's an easy way to know who has sold what to whom.

Let's take a page from the sports industry, particularly auto racing. The racecar drivers, their cars, and their pit crews all display logo patches that advertise their sponsors. It's worth a lot of money to have your company logo on the winner's jacket when the TV cameras roll.

The obvious application to politics: let's require that every elected office holder, at every level – even up to presidents and prime ministers – wear a logo jacket while on duty, with patches denoting the corporations and special interest groups that have put them into office. The bigger the contribution, the bigger the patch.

104

While we're at it, let's include lobbyists as well. Anyone entering or leaving the office of a member of Congress or Parliament – and let's not forget the Defense Department – would have to wear the patches of the special interests they're lobbying for.

But let's not stop there. Each contributor would have to pay for the advertising space on the jackets. In addition to the campaign contributions, they would pay advertising fees, which would go into the public treasury. The money could be used to pay lobbyists to push the interests of all those people and groups who can't afford to hire them.

Would this work?

Are Smart Phones Smart Enough?

It looks like smart phones have become smarter than a lot of the people using them.

Maybe your smart phone should:

> Scold you when you're trying to drive your car and push its buttons at the same time. Professional airline pilots and fighter pilots can't do it – what makes you think you can?

> Remind you that it's bad manners to take or make a call while you're sitting in a seminar, a wedding ceremony, or a church service.

> Advise you that the restaurant that's offering you the discount coupon you just downloaded has lousy food and worse service.

> Block all ill-advised statements, comments, or wisecracks to your spouse or significant other, to keep you out of the dog house. It might be necessary to add a seven-second delay, like the call-in talk shows have, to give the computer time to save your marriage.

> Remind you that you're a pathetic media addict if you pull it out more than once per hour.

Just thinkin'...

"The uncreative mind can spot wrong answers,
but it takes a very creative mind to spot wrong questions."
~ *Antony Jay, business author*

✪ ✪ ✪ ✪ ✪

Is Technology Also Giving Dictators Fits?

How Does One Burn E-books? Hmmm . . .

Where Do Names Come From?

Quite a few English surnames came from the Middle Ages and earlier, when most people were identified by their occupations, e.g. "John the Tailor," or "Giles the Weaver." These trade names morphed into what we know as family names.

Here's a good brain exercise for you: think of as many English names as you can that come from occupations.

Here are a few to get you started:

- o Baker
- o Cook
- o Miller
- o Potter
- o Smith (e.g. "Black-" or "Gold-")
- o Thatcher (one who made thatched roofs)
- o Fowler (one who hunted birds)
- o Sawyer (one who cut wood)

You can take it from there. Try for 50.

"Wherefore Art Thou [Your Name Goes Here]?"

"What's in a name?" asked young Juliet in Shakespeare's famous play *Romeo and Juliet*. "That which we call a rose, by any other name would smell as sweet," she mused.

Well, not actually.

Sales people, advertisers and marketers, political leaders, and con artists have learned, all throughout history, that the name one attaches to a person or an idea can have a huge effect on the way people think about and react to it.

Repetitive brand advertising, for example, seeks to implant an expression, a slogan, or a jingle into as many brains as possible, so that it triggers the desired associations with the product experience. This "brain drool" reaction is so effective and so commonplace in the Western commercial culture that few people notice it or consciously object to it.

- ❖ You're a fan of movie star Tom Cruise? Would you be just as keen about watching someone named Thomas Mapother – his real name?

- ❖ Maybe you liked the classic films starring Norma Jean Mortenson, rechristened by Hollywood marketers as Marilyn Monroe.

- ❖ The same marketers turned Hedwig Eva Maria Kiesler into Hedy Lamarr.

- ❖ Would you pay to see a movie starring a male lead named Marion Morrison? You have, if you've ever watched a John Wayne movie.

- ❖ Are you a fan of the old western movies, many starting Leonard Slye – a.k.a. Roy Rogers?

- ❖ Do you enjoy the movies produced by Allen Konigsberg, a.k.a. Woody Allen?

- ❖ Did you enjoy the vaudeville style of comedy by Nathan Birnbaum, otherwise known as George Burns?

Names have psychological power, if not magical power. In some native cultures, survivors may not speak the name of a member of the tribe who has died, lest they impede his or her soul's journey to the next world.

City leaders in India have reasserted local identity by replacing their British colonial names with the original names: Bombay went back to Mumbai; Bangalore went back to Bengalooru ("the city of boiled beans"); Madras went back to Chennai.

In South Africa, the new black political leadership began replacing some Afrikaaner city names with original tribal names: Pietersburg became Polokwane. Some leaders have advocated a change in the name of the national capital from Pretoria, named after an Afrikaaner hero, to Tshwane, the name of a local chief from pre-colonial days.

What's in a name? A helluva lot, apparently.

Is Technology Making Suicide More Difficult?

Electric cars are eliminating one of the favorite methods of suicide. Seal up your garage, start up your Prius, and wait for the end. You'll wait a long time, so – as they say, "Don't hold your breath."

"Until you make the unconscious conscious,
it will direct your life and you will call it fate."
~ *Carl Jung, Swiss psychologist*

A Woman With Brass Ovaries

I'm planning to set up the Brass Ovaries Award, to recognize women of unusual courage and determination, who have persisted and succeeded against huge challenges.

One of the first candidates will be Mary Bowser, a freed slave who spied for the North during the American Civil War.

She had been raised and educated by a wealthy white family, and set free by the surviving heirs when the patriarch died. The surviving head of the family, Elizabeth Van Lew, was a Quaker and could not reconcile slavery with her spiritual beliefs. Van Lew was prominent in the Richmond upper-crust society, even though she was known as a vocal abolitionist.

Mary Bowser was an unusual person in several ways. One, she had been taught to read and write. Two, she was remarkably intelligent, and made good use of her intellectual capacities in just about everything she did. And three, she had a remarkably retentive memory – some who knew her described her as having a photographic memory.

She remained loyal to Van Lew, who had set up a spying operation against the Confederate government, aiming to speed the decline and fall of the Confederacy, and thereby hasten the abolition of slavery.

Bowser managed to secure a servant's position in the mansion of – none other than – Jefferson Davis, the President of the Confederacy. On a daily basis, as she served food, drinks, and refreshments to Davis and a stream of Confederate officials, she overheard crucial strategic conversations. They spoke freely in her presence, never imagining that a black servant might have any understanding of the political issues and strategic questions they were talking about.

She presented herself as rather dull-witted, and perhaps even somewhat retarded, concealing her intentions behind a plodding attention to her assigned work.

In the privacy of her quarters, she wrote out the key conversations she had listened to, sometimes word for word. When she spotted a document unattended on Davis's desk, she would quickly read it and later write it out from memory.

She passed this information on to Elizabeth Van Lew and her co-conspirators. Much of it became crucially important to Union intelligence experts. Her "fence," or hand-off person for the information, was Thomas McNiven, a local baker who frequently made deliveries to the Davis mansion. She would go out to his wagon to pick up the baked goods, and passed the information to him.

When she realized that Jefferson Davis was beginning to suspect he had a leak, she escaped just before he caught up with her. On the way out, she even tried to burn down his mansion, but didn't succeed.

Details of her later life are obscure, and her personal journal was lost, but her contribution to the destruction of slavery is solidly represented in the history of the Civil War period. The U.S. Government inducted her into the Military Intelligence Hall of Fame.

Monkey See, Monkey Do?

As much as we humans like to believe that we're independent, logical, liberated, practical thinkers, the evidence continues to mount that our behavior is being shaped continuously by signals from our environment that we don't consciously acknowledge.

A few strange examples:

- ❖ In 1997, on July 4, NASA's Mars Rover, the smart go-cart that landed on the red planet and explored its surface, made big news. The Mars Candy Company subsequently reported that sales of its Mars bar shot up dramatically.

- ❖ In a much-publicized news event, the spoiled-princess daughter of a Korean Airlines executive ordered the flight she was on delayed because the attendants served her some macadamia nuts in a bag instead of presenting them on a plate in the style she felt entitled to. The customer outrage and negative news impact led to her demotion. In the ensuing month, e-commerce sites in Korea reported a 20-fold increase in macadamia sales.

Coincidence? Maybe.

Monkey See, Monkey Too?

How much of your behavior is influenced by the signals you pick up unconsciously from your cultural environment?

In the month after Marilyn Monroe took her life, suicide rates in the United States increased by twelve percent; rates went up by ten percent in England and Wales.

Studies of teen-age suicide patterns in America between 1973 and 1979 showed an average increase of about seven percent in the seven-day period following 38 nationally televised stories of suicide.

In 1933 – well before television – a 19 year-old Japanese student, Kiyoko Matsumoto, killed herself by jumping into the thousand foot crater of a volcano on the island of Oshima. The news of her death, and the story of her despair, sparked a bizarre fashion across Japan: in the next few months three hundred young people did the same thing.

Each day about 86 Americans take their lives (not the same 86, of course) and over 1500 attempt it. The suicide rate in Japan is over *100 per day* – more than 36,000 per year – in a country with less than half the population of the U.S.

Although few of us are driven to commit suicide – the ultimate act of self-disapproval – almost all of us are much more susceptible than we think we are to the programming messages we receive from the surrounding culture every day.

There seems to be little doubt that the least well adjusted amongst us take their cues from the entertainment environment. A number of teen-aged mass murderers have modeled their life's drama after the news stories about others of their kind. Social modeling is a primary basis for learning how to behave in various contexts, and the media coverage provides plenty of models for those few deranged individuals who want to make the ultimate statement.

"I who am blind can give one hint to those who see –
one admonition to make full use of the gift of sight:
Use your eyes as if tomorrow you would be stricken blind.
And the same method can be applied to the other senses.
Hear the music of voices, the song of a bird,
the mighty strains of on orchestra,
as if you would be stricken deaf tomorrow.
Touch each object you want to touch as if tomorrow
your tactile sense would fail.
Smell the perfume of flowers, taste with relish each morsel,
as if tomorrow you could never smell and taste again."
~ Helen Keller, American writer and activist

PBI # 14: Honk if You Have Something to Say

The electronic age has promoted the personalization of almost everything. Each of us has his or her individual signature, screen name, email handle, avatar, or web page. We've become a nation of cyber-narcissists.

We even have to have distinctive ringing sounds in our cell phones.

But there's one electronic aspect of our lives that's been holding out – one important part of our identities that hasn't been personalized yet. It's *the automobile horn.*

Most car horns only make one sound. It's hard to communicate much meaning when you can only control the number of beeps and the duration of each beep.

We seem to use our horns mostly for one of two purposes: to warn and to punish. A horn greeting could easily be misunderstood: if you honk at your friend who's crossing the street at the corner, the driver ahead of you might very well assume that you're nagging him or her to get moving. If someone cuts you off in traffic, that one long blast is the only way you have of punishing them for their misdeed.

It seems to me we're long overdue for personalized, customized, individualized car horn sounds. Technologically it would be a snap. And consider the possibilities: sound effects (applause, barking dogs, screeching brakes, police sirens), musical tones, your voice, celebrity voices – pick what you like.

If you see your friend on the street, you can offer him or her a ride. You can politely remind the driver ahead of you that the light has changed. You can flirt with that attractive person who catches your fancy.

Now, I realize the pessimists who read this will immediately think of uses that might cause problems. The sound of gunfire, for example, might not be a wise signal in many situations. Offers to street-race might become a problem. Verbal insults could become contagious. Commercial advertising could add to noise pollution. Flirtation could progress to sexual harassment. Then we might have to have car horn obscenity laws.

But, the way electronic technology is going, it's probably inevitable.

Roman Soldiers

If you were a Roman soldier in the days of the Empire, your main job wouldn't have been fighting other armies. It would have been *stone-working*.

All over the empire, the Roman armies built paved roads, aqueducts, stone walls, forts, coliseums, and god knows what else.

They were good at it, too. A typical aqueduct ran for twenty miles or more, sloping an average of an inch per ten feet, delivering a steady flow of water to the main fountain in a typical city.

Hernias were probably more common amongst Roman soldiers than sword wounds.

One Tough Bugger

There's "tough," and then there's tough.

My nominee for a really tough guy was a 27 year-old Russian scientist, Dr. Leonid Ivanovich Rogozov.

Part of an expedition sent by the Soviet Union to the Antarctic to set up a research field station in 1960, Rogozov developed a life-threatening case of appendicitis early the following year. Without surgery to remove his appendix, he would almost certainly die. But there was no feasible way to get him to any location that had an adequate medical capability.

Fortunately, the 12-man expedition had an experienced surgeon as one of their number.

Unfortunately, Rogozov was the surgeon.

As he experienced the onset of ever-greater pain and threatening symptoms, he decided he would have to remove his own appendix.

He set up a makeshift operating room, with him lying on his bed and his colleagues standing around with the surgical instruments and supplies. He set up a mirror so he could see what he was doing.

A big challenge, however, was mentally reversing the mirror image in his mind, to keep track of where things were inside his abdomen.

Rogozov injected the surgery site with a local anesthetic, which blocked the pain in the neighborhood of the incision, but didn't help to reduce the pain of the disturbance to internal tissues.

He had to pause every few minutes to rest and recover from the pain, and to fight back the weakness and vertigo he was experiencing.

Finally, after almost two hours, he snipped the appendix free from its connection to the intestine, and sewed himself back up.

Looking at the appendix, he realized that, within another 24 hours, it would have ruptured, and he would have been dead.

He recovered from the surgery without incident, and went on to enjoy a long and distinguished career.

The Marx Without a Brother

Karl Heinrich Marx (1818–1883), self-professed advocate of the working stiff, never had a real job in his life.

For most of his adult years he had a wealthy patron, Friedrich Engels – who, by the way, drew an income from his family's capitalist manufacturing operation in England.

Nitwitticisms # 3

"He's either in Afghanistan, or some other country, or dead."
~ *Donald Rumsfeld, U.S. Secretary of Defense*, on the whereabouts of terrorist leader Osama bin Laden

"I feel my best when I'm happy."
~ *Actress Winona Ryder*

"Quite frankly, teachers are the only profession that teach our children."
~ *U.S. President George W. Bush*

"I haven't committed a crime. What I did was fail to comply with the law."
~ *Donald Dinkins, former New York City Mayor*, accused of not paying his income tax

"I was a pilot flying an airplane and it just so happened that where I was flying made what I was doing spying."
~ *Francis Gary Powers*, pilot of U-2 spy plane shot down over the Soviet Union

"Smoking kills. If you're killed, you've lost a very important part of your life."
~ *Actress Brooke Shields*, during an interview to become spokesperson for a federal anti-smoking campaign

"Free health care is just that, free health care, until you get sick. Then, if you get sick and you don't get health care, you die and you don't vote. It's actually a pretty clever system. Take care of the people who can vote and people who can't vote, get rid of them as quickly as possible by not giving them care so they can't vote against you. That's how it works."

~ U.S. Senator Rick Santorum

To Be or Not to Be

If you were a part of speech, or a punctuation mark, which one would you be?

Buckminster Fuller, the science philosopher and deep thinker said, "As I think about how I operate in the world, I seem to be a verb."

Make what you like of his metaphor.

I've wondered about that myself. My conclusion:

I seem to be an ampersand.

"The best captain does not plunge headlong
Nor is the best soldier a fellow hot to fight.
The greatest victor wins without the battle."

~ Lao Tzu, ancient Chinese philosopher

The Good Book's Good Enough for Them

> 4h   **Two state representatives in Mississippi proposed making the Bible the state's official book.**
> The Associated Press *

For them, apparently, old-time religion and old-time politics are one and the same.

My Restaurant Rant

Why is it so goddamn difficult to have tables in restaurants and coffee shops that sit flat on the floor, without wobbling?

115

The customers have to crawl under the table and put wadded-up napkins under the too-high leg, so they won't spill their coffee every time they bump the table. Real high-tech.

And, by the way, here's a little tip for the people who run restaurants: when your customers have to raise their hands up to shoulder level to eat their food, either the table is too high or the seat is too low. The standard distance from the top of the seat to the top of the table is 9.5 inches.

What's so friggin' hard about that?

The (Only) Ten Basic News Stories

Lots of people consider the news industry cynical and committed to pandering to the lowest common intellectual denominator. But few have noticed the curious irony that lies at the very core of the news paradigm. This irony may offer a better explanation of why the news is the way it is than any speculations about the ethics and motives of the news producers.

The curious irony is that, in this so-called "Third-Wave" age of information, as futurist Alvin Toffler named it, the commercial news process is actually imprisoned in a Second-Wave model, i.e. an industrial model of news production.

Any subject expert who is regularly called upon to appear in news cameos (such as I am, as a business consultant) soon discerns the unmistakable factory-like hum of the news operation. The process by which video editors interweave the live performances of news readers, the cutaways to remote units at the crime scene or the lawn of the White House, the obligatory establishing shot of the professor walking across campus to the laboratory, and the stock footage (the Rodney King beating, the Clinton-Lewinsky hug, or the lab technician testing the DNA samples) pays little homage to Toffler's Third Wave concept.

Instead, it's straight out of the Industrial Age. Probably the closest product analogy to the news is a fast-food operation, something like making hamburgers or baking pastries.

Each little piece of news rolls down the line like a tidy, production-controlled PopTart (with due respect to Kellogg's popular product): flavored, sweetened, glazed, and baked to perfection.

Whatever the sacrifice in depth or insight, the fast-food news model is undeniably efficient and remarkably cost-effective.

What makes any industrial production process efficient and cost-effective is the use of *standard products*. In the news industry this translates into a few well-proven, reliable story structures. A basic inventory of about ten standard news stories makes the process of baking the news easy to manage.

One can tune to virtually any news show, from CNN's breaking news, to financial news, to the local stations, and see a mix of these ten basic PopTarts rolling by in a varied sequence. This standard-product paradigm probably does more to explain the universal sameness of news programming, virtually around the world, than any supposed ideology or motivational premise.

Perhaps those who criticize news producers as being cynical, exploitive, and shallow are right, but for the wrong reasons. They may be less the conscious purveyors of intellectual pabulum than they are helpless prisoners locked in their own PopTart factories. It's hard to give up such a comfortable way of doing business, and it's easy to rationalize: "People like our PopTarts."

What are the ten basic PopTarts – er, sorry, new stories? Just about anybody can tick them off, with a bit of thought. Here they are, for the record.

1. *Shock and Horror.* As they say in the news biz, "If it bleeds, it leads." Murders, especially multiples, acts of unusual violence, brutality, or sadism, shark attacks, and the carnage left by explosions are sure fire grabbers for the attention of a nation of gawkers.

2. *Tragedy.* Preferably enhanced by the horror factor, as in a suicide bombing, the Tragedy category includes natural disasters, airplane crashes, and hotel fires. The more lives that are wrecked, the better the material for the mike-in-the-face victim vignettes and the human interest stories about how the brave victims are "trying to put the pieces of their lives back together."

3. *Hot Sex.* This is a plentiful product line, virtually addictive for news producers. It ranges from the intimate lives of celebrities to "socially responsible" stories about teen-agers having oral sex. It also includes derivative

pornography, such as stories about the exotic dancers at the local club who are fighting to unionize. The story wouldn't be complete without the drop-in shots of pole dancers and the interviews with busty entertainers.

4. *Scandal.* Best teamed up with the Hot Sex story, for double effect, the misdeeds of government officials or corporate bigwigs allow us all to cluck our tongues and enjoy seeing the sinners embarrassed and properly chastised.

5. *The Fall of the Mighty.* Watching powerful people get knocked off their high horses has a special appeal, and could almost qualify as a national pastime. Combine a Fall of the Mighty story with good Scandal, add a great Hot Sex story, and you have a grand slam. A head of state gets thrown out for having sex with the wrong person and trying to cover it up: it don't get no better'n 'at.

6. *Conflict.* Just as people will always stop and gawk at a fist-fight, whether in the schoolyard or in Taiwan's Parliament chamber, conflict and the imminence of physical violence will always arrest attention. War is probably the most reliable news product of all; it always has been. In a polite society, violence is replaced by conflict between political parties, or among advocacy groups pursuing various social agendas. Newsbakers will nearly always introduce an element of conflict into a story if they can figure out how. It's kind of a basic ingredient, like sugar or salt.

7. *Worry.* Journalists seem to suffer from a constitutional aversion to being perceived as naive or overly optimistic. As a result, they seem compelled to find the dark side of just about any issue; the cynical motive, the reasons why it's too good to be true, and the looming possibility that something could go seriously wrong. Some economists have contended that more recessions are caused by journalists warning about recessions than by the business cycle. It is their sworn duty to help us worry about things like the possibility that the earth might collide with an asteroid within the next 1,000 years.

8. *Voyeurism.* The bizarre, the perverted, the weird, the sick and twisted, and the deviant, all make good entertainment for gawkers. The suicide jumper, the hostage standoff, the

execution, and the demented old lady living with the 300 cats, all provide an element of curiosity or excitement which many people apparently need in their lives. In some cases, as with TV shows in the "bubba" genre, many people seem to enjoy peering at other people whose lives are clearly more screwed up than their own.

9. *Dilemmas.* Newsbakers love stories about conflicts that can't be solved. The abortion issue, cloning, capital punishment, euthanasia, and the right to die, all arouse strong feelings and polarize opinion. The conflict ingredient comes for free, and "balanced coverage" is easy to claim. The frequent use of two-sided Moral Dilemma stories helps perpetuate the myth of "objective journalism."

10. *Gee-Whiz Stories.* And finally, we need a change-of-pace product, so we won't get the idea they're constantly pandering to our darker natures. This can take many forms, but usually has to be a novelty segment, a curiosity piece, or a heart-warmer. The local spelling bee, the dog that rescues the baby, astronauts in space, the Olympic athlete's mom crying tears of joy, and the President's hemorrhoids all help to round out the product offering and let us know that news people are actually regular folks like the rest of us.

So, before we get too pious about the quality of journalism, let's remember that all products have to find receptor sites on the neurons of their intended customers, or they won't survive in the marketplace. Just as fast food products find a strong and reliable response, fast news products arrest the attention of enough people long enough to sell them the fast food. Those of us who perceive the news as a mediocre type of information product aren't really the intended customers – for the news or the fast food.

Talk About Being "Out of the Loop!"

American Vice Presidents have been, for most of the country's history, little more than miscellaneous figures. Many of them had little or nothing to do with the running of the country. Many served with presidents they barely knew and seldom even met.

The U.S. Constitution has very little to say about the position of VP, and suggests that the only function of the person holding that job is to stand by, ready to take over if the president dies or is incapacitated.

Most VPs have been paired with their presidential partners for the sole purpose of attracting votes from certain geographic regions or political factions. Abe Lincoln's first VP was a complete nobody named Hannibal Hamlin, a name completely unfamiliar to modern Americans. His second-term VP was Andrew Johnson, who visited Washington only occasionally, and stayed in a modest hotel the few times he was there.

Harry Truman, who took over as President when Franklin D. Roosevelt died three months into his fourth term, barely knew FDR, and had only met with him privately a few times after taking office.

Truman had been a typical candidate of convenience during the election, chosen only because he was a political nonentity who would not draw fire from any faction. He seldom attended cabinet meetings, and was almost never consulted on key issues.

Amazingly – or, maybe, not surprisingly – Truman knew absolutely nothing of the Manhattan Project, the gigantic and extremely expensive venture to produce the atomic bomb, even though it spanned several years and employed thousands of scientists at a number of sites. The first time Truman heard about "The Bomb" was the day he walked into the Oval Office to take over as President.

"Don't saw the limb you're sitting on,

unless they're trying to hang you from it."

~ *Stanislaw J. Lee, American satirist*

Try Your Hand at Some Poetry

Language constantly amazes me. Think about poems like the Japanese haiku, that have exactly 17 syllables, usually arranged in three lines of five, seven, and then five. As strict as the physical arrangement of the words is, they still convey elegant philosophical messages.

An old poem by Adelaide Crapsey gave me the idea to try something similar, with the first line having one word, and each of the following lines adding one more word respectively.

Modified this way, her original verse gave rise to:

Now

These be

Three silent things:

The gently falling snow;

The hour just before dawn;

The lips of one just dead.

Reference: "Three Silent Things," by Adelaide Crapsey

PBI # 15: Do We Really Want Free Will?

Maybe we're allowed to think we have free will, even though we don't?

Or, maybe the only thing we have free will about is whether to believe we have free will?

Or, . . .

Love Means Never Saying . . .

Ah, those three little words – the ones that no man ever really wants to hear a woman say:

"Is it in?"

Now, *There's* a Show With Legs

Theater people like to refer to a show that runs successfully for a long time as one that has "legs."

The longest running play of all time is "The Mousetrap," a clever murder mystery by Agatha Christie.

The Mousetrap opened in London's West End in 1952, and has been running continuously since then. It reached its 25,000th performance on 18 November 2012.

It's also known for its surprise ending, which the cast members traditionally ask the audience not to reveal.

"Each snowflake in an avalanche pleads its innocence."

~ *Stanislaw J. Lee, American satirist*

Colonies on the Moon

If we ever put colonies on the moon, won't it just be a replay of the way we colonized Earth?

- ❖ Countries from Earth would fight to get the best land.

- ❖ They'd have wars over who should control the colonies.

- ❖ The colonies would fight with one another over resources.

- ❖ The people living in the colonies would want their independence.

- ❖ After they revolted and became independent, they'd have the usual civil wars.

So, what would be new? Same old shit, different orbit.

Favorite Lame Joke # 6

The parish priest was sitting at his kitchen table one afternoon, working on his sermon for the coming Sunday.

It had been raining heavily for several days, and the dam up the river from the village had given way, flooding the town and driving all of the parishioners out of their homes.

He looked out the window and saw the waters rising to the edge of his window sill. He saw people swimming about in the flood waters, rowing boats, and clinging to anything they could find that would float.

Just then two people in a boat came by his window. "Father, jump into the boat with us and we'll get you to safety."

The priest waved them on. "No, no thank you. I'll be fine. Just be on your way and look after yourselves."

"Father," they implored him, "do come with us. It isn't safe here."

"No, no," said the priest. "Off you go – I'll be fine."

"Well, please yourself," they said and they rowed away.

As the water continued to rise, the priest gathered up his papers and moved upstairs to his study.

The water continued to rise menacingly. As he looked out his window, several more people came by in a large rowboat.

"Father, please – get in the boat with us. We'll take you to safety."

Still quite calm, the priest said "No, my children. God will look after me. You go on and save yourselves – I'll be fine."

He'd have none of their pleading, so they finally gave up and went off in their boat.

The waters kept rising to the point where he had to climb up onto the roof. There he was, holding on to the weather vane, when a third boat came by.

"Father, you must come with us. This is a very dangerous situation; please get in the boat and save yourself. It's your last chance!"

With great calm and magnanimity he waved them on. "No, no – I'll be fine. I have my faith in the Lord. He will save me from the flood."

Distraught but unable to dislodge his simple faith, they went on.

Unfortunately, his strategy didn't work. He drowned, and the next thing he knew he was standing at the Pearly Gates. St. Peter spotted him and called out "So – there you are!"

The priest, looking astonished, raised his hands in confusion and disbelief. "What happened?" he implored. "Why did God not save me from the flood? I've lived a virtuous life, I've devoted my whole life to the service of the Church – I thought God would save me!"

St. Peter shrugged his shoulders and said, "What are you talking about? We sent three boats for you."

I often think about that little story and its implications for the opportunities and options that life presents to us. Several of my colleagues and I often use it as a metaphorical shorthand when discussing potential business opportunities: "Do you think this might be a 'boat' we're looking at?"

The Worst War for American Deaths

Question: Of all the wars that American soldiers have fought and died in, which one do you think cost the most American lives?

Answer: the Civil War.

Estimates put total American deaths for all conflicts at about 1.26 million, a small fraction of the deaths suffered by the other major nations.

Historians record a total of about 626,000 deaths in the four-year Civil War.

Prior to the Vietnam War, deaths from the American Civil War outnumbered deaths from all the major wars put together.

The bloodshed has seldom been equaled. One three-day battle, at Gettysburg, killed nearly as many men as the entire Vietnam conflict.

And, bear in mind that they were not fighting with modern machine guns, automatic rifles, planes, drones, or missiles. They did it with single-shot muzzle-loading muskets, bayonets, and primitive cannon.

"If a man of sufficiently complex mind

persists long enough in a perverse course of action,

he can eventually succeed in kicking his own ass

out the door and into the street."

~ *A.J. Liebling, American journalist*, who offered Liebling's Law (paraphrased)

The Tyranny of Two

Here's something to think about . . .

Recent research suggests that our brains may be pre-wired for *dichotomized* thinking. That's a fancy name for thinking and perceiving in terms of two – and only two – opposing possibilities.

These research findings might help explain how and why the public discourse of our culture has become so polarized and rancorous, and how we might be able to replace it with a more intelligent conversation.

Neurologists have explored the activity of certain key regions of the human forebrain – the *frontal lobe* – trying to understand how the brain switches between tasks. Scientists generally accept the idea that the brain can only consciously manage one task at a time, notwithstanding the claim that today's youngsters excel at multi-tasking.

However, some researchers are now suggesting that our brains can keep tabs on two tasks at a time, by "bookmarking" each one to a different side of the brain. Apparently, we toggle back and forth, with one task being primary and the other on standby.

Add a third task, however, and one of the others has to drop off the to-do list. Scans of brain activity during this task switching have led to the hypothesis that the brain actually likes handling things in pairs. Indeed, the brain itself is subdivided into two distinct half-brains, or hemispheres.

Some researchers are now extending this reasoning to suggest that the brain has a built-in tendency, when confronted by complex propositions, to selfishly reduce the set of choices to just two. Apparently it doesn't like to work very hard.

Considering how quickly most of us make our choices and set our opinions, it's unlikely that all of the options will even be identified, never mind carefully considered.

One of our popular clichés is "Well, there are two sides to every story." Why only two? Maybe the less sophisticated and less rational members of our society are caught up in *duplex thinking*, because the combination of a polarized brain and unexamined emotional reflexes keeps them there.

Our popular vocabulary constantly signals this dichotomizing mental habit: "Are you with us, or against us?" "If you're not part of the solution, you're part of the problem."

Some will protest, "But it's obvious that duality is a fundamental aspect of nature. There's day, and there's night." (And what about the two twilights?) "There are two sexes – males and females." (And what about transgender, homosexual, and gender-ambiguous persons?) "Any game of sport has winners and losers." (And most can also have ties, stalemates, and rained-out games.) "You're alive or you're dead – there's no in–between." (And what about a person who's in a vegetative state and on life support?)

Our mental malfunction, as I see it, is not in considering the polarities – which we must inevitably do. It's in drifting toward a habit of thinking that casts aside the diverse alternatives and variations, and refers all of our experience to one of two extremes.

Imagination, creativity, and innovation all thrive in the "twilight zone," not at the poles of opinion.

Curiously, part of our cranial craving for two-ness might be related to our own physiology: the human body is *bilaterally symmetrical*. Draw an imaginary center line down through the front of a person and you see a lot of parts (not all, of course), that come in pairs: two eyes, two ears, two nostrils, matching teeth on left and right sides, two shoulders, two arms, two hands, two nipples, two legs, two knees, and two feet. Inside you'll find two of some things and one of others.

Again, our common language encodes the effect of this anatomical self-reference. "On the one hand, there is X. But on the other hand, we have Y." Many people describe political views as being either "left" or "right."

Literature through the ages, as well the rhetoric of empire building, warfare, commerce, and modern politics have reflected the "good guys and bad guys" motif. "We're going to win because God is on our side."

If we Cro-Magnons had evolved with three arms and hands, or more, would we habitually think and talk in terms of several "hands?" Maybe there would be "three sides to every story?"

If it's likely that any one person's brain will tend to throw options overboard until it settles on a comfortable pair, then certainly our newsbakers have made dichotomizing a religious sacrament.

The popular press routinely constructs "news" stories around conflicts and differences between pairs of opposing people, factions, and ideologies. Bipolar conflict is the very essence of most of the news.

Option fatigue can affect all of us. During the 2004 U.S. presidential election, an unusually large slate of Democrats lined up to compete for the job. The Republicans had already anointed incumbent President George Bush, Jr., as their guy, so the newsbakers had to quickly boil down the competition to one candidate per side. They simply didn't have the collective attention span to follow or report on so many candidates.

The press coverage immediately began to marginalize all except a small handful of the Democrats, and the unrelenting mantra of the news became "Who's going to drop out next?"

Okay, so we're predisposed to polarize. And not all polarization is dysfunctional – a lot of it is necessary and useful. The question presents: how can we improve our thinking and reacting, so as to liberate ourselves from the extremes of dichotomization? Are there some simple mental tricks that can keep us thinking creatively? Here are a few:

> *Have fewer opinions.* The Arabic philosopher Rumi reportedly advised, "If you seek to understand a thing, be neither for nor against."

> *Keep your opinions and conclusions on probation.* Think of an opinion as a home-made theory – a temporary and limited interpretation of what you've perceived, open to improvement as better information becomes available.

> *Let go of the need to be certain about everything.* Train yourself to be comfortable with a certain amount of ambiguity, "not-sure-ness," and the possibility of other valuable perspectives you haven't considered.

> *Seek the "third hand"* – and any other "hands" you can discover. Ask yourself, and others, "Are there other options to be considered?"

➤ *Modify your language.* Replace the word "but" with "and" as often as you can, even if it sounds weird at first. Practice it for a while and you might find yourself thinking differently in addition to talking differently. Try substituting "and" for "or" in some instances – to suggest that there might be multiple options, not just two.

➤ *Remind yourself every day that your "truth" is not the same as any other person's truth.* As much as we enjoy that self-righteous feeling of declaring ourselves correct – in our own minds and world-views – all truth is local to the brains in which it resides.

➤ *Avoid head-butting contests with opinionated people.* When you get drawn into a debate, and you take a position that's the polar opposite of the other person's position, all you're doing is reinforcing their entrenchment. If you want them to discover your truth, why would you want to build resistance in them? Better to steer around the argument and make the sale another time or in another way.

Use Your (Bald) Head

It's hip for men to be bald these days, even if they still own a lot of hair.

But now that so many guys are shaving their domes, naturally you'll have to go further, if you want to be hipper than the next guy.

How? Use that bald surface in more creative ways:

❖ Put on a coat of silver paint and let other people use it as a mirror; be a considerate guy.

❖ Tattoo useful information there that might be interesting to eligible ladies, such as your penis size, your annual income, your cell phone number – that sort of stuff.

❖ Install a solar cell in your scalp and use the electricity to power your wearable electronics.

You get the idea. Now think up your own possibilities.

Factoids # 4

* Average life span of a major league baseball: 7 pitches.

* Average number of people airborne over the U.S. during any given hour: 61,000.

* Babies are born without kneecaps. They start with little pads of cartilage, which ossify by the time they're about 2–6 years old.

* By artistic tradition, if a public statue of a person on a horse has both of the horse's front legs in the air, the person died in battle; if the horse has one front leg in the air, the person died as a result of wounds received in battle; if the horse has all four legs on the ground, the person died of natural causes. Not all sculptors have felt obligated to this tradition.

* In 10 minutes, a large hurricane releases more energy than all the world's nuclear weapons combined.

* An important purpose of the U.S. interstate highway system, begun by President Eisenhower during the peak of the Cold War, was to permit mass evacuations of the cities, as well as easy movement of military forces. The design required that one mile in every five would be straight, for use as airstrips if necessary. The official name was the National Defense Highway System. The construction of the superhighways, the availability of cheap gasoline, and massive motivational advertising by American carmakers, permanently shifted the U.S. transport infrastructure away from trains and toward individual cars.

* The first testicular guard, the "Cup," reportedly was used in Hockey in 1874, and helmets came into wide use by 1974. That means it only took 100 years for men to decide that brains and balls are equally important.

How to Get Elected in Ecuador

The people of a small town in Ecuador elected a can of foot powder as their mayor. I'm not making this up.

During the 1967 mayoral election in the small Ecuadorian town of Picoaza, with about 4,000 inhabitants, a pharma company began advertising its product, Pulvapies. Their creative ad types decided to spoof the election as an attention getting strategy.

Their billboards and mailers carried the slogan, "Vote for any candidate, but if you want well-being and hygiene, vote for Pulvapies." They even distributed a leaflet disguised as a campaign ad, saying, "For Mayor: Honorable Pulvapies."

Most of the voters, semi-literate and thoroughly confused, marked their ballots for Pulvapies as a write-in candidate. When the votes were counted, Pulvapies had trounced all the others.

That left the national election commission trying to figure out what to do, and the losing candidates threatening to sue the company.

Ah, yes, democracy at work . . .

"Toward no crimes have men shown themselves so cold-bloodedly cruel as in punishing differences in belief."

~ *James Russell Lowell, American essayist*

Cornpone Opinions

Mark Twain quoted his boyhood friend Jerry, a young slave who was wise well beyond his years, as saying,

"You tell me whar a man gits his cornpone, en' I'll tell you what his 'pinions is."

PBI # 16: Is Your Grandma Wearing a Bomb?

Airport security screening procedures are as illogical and ineffective as they are inconvenient. Why scan and search hundreds of thousands of innocent people every day, just to identify a very small handful of potential bombers?

There's a simpler way. Turn each security gate into a bomb detection chamber. After being properly warned, each person would step into the chamber and push a button. If he or she were wearing or carrying explosives, or had ingested them, pushing the button would detonate them. No explosion, no explosives – please proceed to the boarding gate.

There would be the obvious issues of disposal, recycling the chamber and getting it ready for the next test, and all that, but nothing technologically difficult. It could even be linked into the airline's seat assignment system. Standby passengers would automatically move up one notch on the waiting list.

Ideologically, it might be less than satisfying for the bomber, but that's not a legitimate security concern. It might even have a deterrent effect: does the bomber still get the 72 virgins when he gets to heaven, even if he hasn't killed anybody else? Or maybe he just gets a dozen. If he's been paid, does his family have to give the money back? Who gets the refund on his ticket?

All great solutions have their little details to be worked out, of course.

Is it Time to De-criminalize Sex?

Outlawing prostitution is a relatively modern social practice. Most ancient cultures, so far as I am aware – at least the pre-Christian ones – treated it as an ordinary form of commerce. Western societies have demonized it and prosecuted it for so long that it has become a taken-for-granted part of our moral and legal codes. But longevity doesn't make it any more sensible or logical.

The principle seems to be: you can charge a person money to do an unimaginable range of intimate things to his or her body, *except giving them an orgasm*. You can cut their hair, drill holes in their teeth, remove parts of their body, enlarge other parts, vacuum fat from under their skin, encase them in mud, rearrange their bones and joints, massage them, carve indelible pictures onto their skin – but you can't give them an orgasm for pay.

You can do it for free, but if they pay you to do it, you can both go to jail.

I don't get it.

131

I Fear Journalists More Than Terrorists

There is no creature on the planet more dangerous than a journalist who's found a statistic.

The Paradoxical Power of Humility

Humility is widely underrated in most Western cultures, it seems to me. It's also widely misunderstood – maybe that's why it's underrated.

Our popular-media culture is saturated with themes of conflict, combat, and conquest. Popular films feature cops chasing crooks; the military fighting terrorists; the lone avenger pursuing the evil-doers. We say we love peacemakers, but our heroes are warriors. As a society, we like our celebrities to be cheeky, self-important, and even a bit narcissistic.

Little wonder that humble people seem sort of strange to us, as if they're following some syncopated life rhythm that few people around them quite "get."

Having claimed that humility is misunderstood, I suppose it's incumbent on me to offer a definition.

What is humility? It's a subtle concept, and I find myself having to frame it mostly in terms of what it's not. My conception of humility is what you have when you give up certain self-magnifying thought patterns, reflexes, and behaviors. I offer the proposition – and the value judgment – that humility is a kind of liberation, a *paradoxical state of freedom* from the culturally imposed norms of narcissistic "me-first" thinking.

Practitioners of many spiritual traditions, such as Buddhism, would say that attaining such a state is a necessary part of the journey toward enlightenment.

One definition of humility is:

132

a psycho-social orientation characterized by 1) a sense of emotional autonomy; and 2) freedom from the control of the "competitive reflex."

What is the competitive reflex? It is:

the preconscious, visceral impulse to oppose or outdo others, or to auto-react against perceived threats to one's established sense of self.

Consonant with the premise of what humility is not, as I think of it:

- It's not letting others "push you around."
- It's not being a doormat, a sucker, or letting people "walk all over you."
- It's not constantly sacrificing your interests to those of others (and then feeling like a victim or a martyr).
- It's not avoiding conflict or confrontation – not of your making, anyway – for the sake of "being nice."
- It's not about hiding your feelings or suppressing your views to avoid alienating others.

Humility is about emotional neutrality. It involves an experience of growth in which you no longer need to put yourself above others, but you don't put yourself below them, either. Everyone is your peer – from the most "important" person to the least. You're just as valuable as every other human being on the planet, no more and no less. It's about behaving and reacting from purposes, not emotions. You learn to simply disconnect or de-program the competitive reflex in situations where it's not productive.

The legendary gestalt therapist Fritz Perls said,

"I am I, and you are you; I am not in this world to live up to your expectations, and you are not in this world to live up to mine."

It's a liberating idea, I believe.

So, how do you free yourself from the competitive reflex? That requires, first, that you recognize the reflex when it rises up in you; and second, that you choose a more versatile response.

How aware are you of the competitive reflex in yourself?

Let's take an example. Your friend has just remodeled her home, and is pleased and proud of the results. She invites you in to have a look. The premise of the situation, whether your recognize it or not, is for her to show off her house; for you to appreciate it and praise her for it; and for her to feel good about it. So what do you do?

As she proudly points out the various features, do you feel an impulse to tell her how she could have done it better? Do you "explain" things to her, signaling that you know more about these things than she does? Do you straighten that picture that's slightly askew? Do you discourse on how you did it better in your own home? Does it turn into a bragging contest, with two people trying to score points on each other? Or do you help her enjoy her moment of triumph, satisfaction, and self-congratulation?

There's a long list of such diagnostic test questions. Do you offer unsolicited advice to others about how to live their lives better? Do you "damn with faint praise" when somebody shares their new idea or new discovery about life? If someone tells a joke, do you feel compelled to top it with a better one? Or, do you hold back on laughing, so the joke falls flat? Do you always have a better story, a better example, a better suggestion, or a better solution? Do you feel compelled to demonstrate your smart you are, or how much you know?

Are you a back seat driver? Do you like to tell people how to raise their kids better? Do you lecture or preach to others? When someone says something that's mistaken or misinformed, how to you react? If you have a different opinion, do you precipitate a win-lose debate, or do you show respect for the other person's view as you're sharing your own?

Humility is less a matter of self-restraint and more a matter of self-esteem. The greater your sense of self-worth, the easier it is to appreciate others, to praise them, and to encourage them.

Does this mean that it's wrong to try to win at bridge, or improve your tennis game, or compete to get ahead in your work place? Of course not – those are parts of a separate dimension of life. Your talents and abilities will speak for themselves. What we're dealing with here is a matter of *social intelligence*, which involves inviting people to move with and toward you, instead of away and against you.

A well-developed sense of humility shines through in your behavior toward others. They feel affirmed, appreciated, encouraged, validated, and psychically nourished. Most of us are powerfully drawn to people who treat us that way, like bees to flowers.

The esteemed psychologist William James reminded us,

> "The deepest craving in all human beings is the desire to be appreciated."

> "There is a quality in a few unique individuals which
> I can only best describe as acceptance.
> In the presence of such persons, I feel safe, at home,
> and eager to share and learn. Their attitude toward life is
> gentle and affirming, and this in turn brings out the best and the deepest in me,
> and makes me feel, somehow, capable of all the good
> I have ever hoped to accomplish."
> - Alex Noble

What's Whack?

The English language amazes me and amuses me. For example:

What the hell is "whack?"

I hear people say things like, "My computer is out of whack." Or, "Our accounting system is out of whack."

So, when it's fixed, is it then "in whack?" "Back in whack?"

Can you put it back in whack by whacking it with your fist?

Doesn't seem right . . .

Stop Telling Me to "Be in the Now"

That's one of those hip, pop-psych expressions these days. "Be in the now." "Be here now." "Be in the here and now." (Can you be in the now, but not the here? The here, but not the now?) You can buy books with titles like "The Power of Now."

There's only one small problem with this: there is no "now."

Think about it for a second (a second is longer than a now). Now is an imaginary figment of the human brain – it's an instant in the flow of time that has no duration.

Try this on somebody, the next time they ask "What time is it?" You can say "Now?" and they'll say, "Yes, now." Then you say, "Do you mean now, as when you first asked me, or the now I asked you about, or *right now*?" Of course, by the time they can answer, "right now" is already gone and it's another now.

What most people think of as now is just the first instant of the future.

"I'm all for progress, but it's been going on far too long."

~ *Ogden Nash, American humorist*

PBI # 17: Killing 'em Softly

Even without the humanitarian issues, or questions of compassion, the death penalty seems to be one of our crazier cultural institutions. So much about it is illogical and unreal.

For example, when they administer a lethal injection, do they still swab the guy's arm with alcohol to make sure it doesn't get infected?

What if the inmate had a heart attack on the way to the execution chamber? Would they resuscitate him, or just let the heart attack do the job? If they resuscitate him, how long would they allow him to convalesce until he's ready to be killed?

As the time for an inmate's execution approaches, they usually place him on "suicide watch," to make sure he doesn't try to kill himself. What's the point? If he asked to be allowed to commit suicide, would they let him?

Actually, that suicide option might make a lot of sense – at least economically. In the U.S., it takes anywhere from 15 to 25 years after sentencing to execute a person for a capital crime. The cost of keeping someone in prison, at maximum security, for that long is well over a million dollars.

Suppose they offered the death-row inmate a "buy-out" option – sort of like buying out a contract or paying a worker to retire early? Let's say the offer is $100,000, payable in cash, in exchange for an agreement to commit suicide within a year. The inmate could walk out of prison with a tracking chip installed in his (or her) body, and have a grand spree spending the "termination bonus" – not violating any laws, of course.

When the "deadline" arrived, he'd check in to a suicide clinic, or if he tried to flee, the job could be done remotely by electronic signal.

As a matter of fact, maybe a lot of inmates serving life sentences might be interested in that kind of an offer. Maybe the warden could offer them different options for killing themselves.

Just trying to save the taxpayers some money . . .

Some Useful Advice

"Never pick a fight with people who buy ink by the barrel."
~ *Attributed to various public personalities*, most likely said first by William I. Greener Jr., U.S. presidential press aide.

"Never slap a man who's chewing tobacco."
~ *Will Rogers*

"Don't squat with spurs on."
~ *Will Rogers*

"Never eat at any place called Mom's;
Never play poker with any guy named 'Doc';
And never sleep with a woman who has more problems than you do."
~ *Anonymous*

How to Get Straight A's in Life

In a dinner conversation with a colleague, we got to exploring the kinds of attitudes that kids need to acquire for success in life. We were talking about her granddaughter, who is raising several very savvy kids, in the midst of difficult circumstances.

I asked, "If you could pick out one absolutely key attitude that you would advise her to instill in the kids, what would it be?"

She couldn't settle on just one, so we started making an inventory list. I noticed that all of attitudes that first jumped into her mind had names beginning with "A."

Authority: claiming for one's self the power to act, interact, and transact with others from one's own values, purposes, and intentions; acting from the "place of cause," rather than being "at effect"; refusing to be a victim, a martyr, a pawn, or a push-over.

Autonomy: owning one's sense of self; freeing one's self from emotional oppression, manipulation, or control by others; letting go of primitive, reflexive emotions such as guilt, shame, envy, jealousy, hate, revenge, and resentment; freeing one's self from the programming of the surrounding society – what Abraham Maslow referred to as *resistance to enculturation*.

Authenticity: staying true to yourself; standing by your beliefs; living up to the values you set for yourself; keeping your word; doing what you say you will do; "doing business" honestly and openly with others; being willing to sacrifice the convenience of the easy way when it's time to stand up and do the right thing.

Accountability: having and following an inner standard for one's own actions; acknowledging, accepting, and learning from one's mistakes, rather than rationalizing or trying to displace them to others; self-accountability is far more important than accountability to other people or systems.

Adaptability: letting go of the need to be certain about everything, the need to be perfect, and the need to always be right; learning to forgive yourself for making mistakes; being willing to listen to others and learn from them; realizing that most problems have more than one right answer; keeping your opinions permanently on probation; understanding that each person has his or her own truth, and that what's true for one person might not be true for another.

Are we teaching our kids how to get "straight A's" in life? For that matter, how many of us adults truly understand and behave from the A-attitudes? Are our schools capable of doing it? Are parents and families capable of doing it? Or shall we continue to leave the most important life-lessons to chance?

"My mother never saw the irony in calling me a son-of-a-bitch."

~ *Jack Nicholson, American character actor*

An Example of Cruelty to Children

An American clergyman named *Maltbie D. Babcock* wrote a number of popular hymns for singing in church.

Now, I ask you: What kind of a sadist names his child "Maltbie?"

A Bit of Folk Wisdom

There's little education in the second kick of a mule.

~ *Anonymous*

Did Ancient Astronauts Build the Pyramids?

Various theories have been advanced to explain the construction of the colossal Egyptian pyramids, which date back as far as 5,000 years.

The popular notion that the builders had help from ancient visitors from outer space has always seemed pretty far-fetched.

However, there's no real viable alternative to the fanciful explanations. Scientists still speculate and debate about how it could have been done – presumably without electricity, without power tools, without explosives, and primarily using brute labor.

Run the numbers:

The Great Pyramid of Cheops, at the Giza site, has an estimated 2.5 million blocks of stone, each about half the size of a modern automobile.

Archaeologists generally posit that the construction went on for twenty years or more. That comes out to 175,200 hours, or 10,512,000 minutes.

To calculate the amount of time allowed to set each stone into place, just divide the number of minutes by 2.5 million stones. You get about 4 minutes per stone.

Could ancient builders lay 2.5 million stones at a rate of one every four minutes, non-stop, 24/7, for 20 years? It sounds rather difficult.

Even supposing the construction took 100 years (much longer than the lifespan of the pharaoh who was to be buried in it), that's still one stone every 20 minutes. Still a tall order.

While you're noodling those numbers, consider the challenge of illuminating the work site during the hours of darkness, so the workers could see well enough to position the stones very accurately.

Then consider that the Great Pyramid is aligned to the north-south axis of the earth to within one degree.

That ain't easy.

A Simple Moral Truth

Lord Charles Bowen, the British judge and legal scholar, observed (variously quoted):

"The rain falls from above,

on the just and the unjust fella;

but more upon the just, you see,

for the unjust has the just's umbrella."

Molest Me, Please

I would never make light of the experiences of children and teens who are abused by adults they depend on, such as teachers or sports coaches. That's a terrible experience to have inflicted on a person, especially at a vulnerable age.

But – just sayin' – when I was sitting there in ninth grade science class, admiring Ms. Esmont's cute buns as she was writing on the chalkboard, if she had offered me a roll in the hay, I'm not really sure I'd have felt that I had been molested.

It's Official: Transgender is OK in Thailand

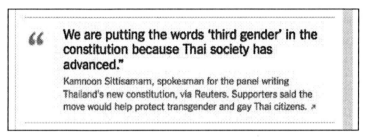

> **We are putting the words 'third gender' in the constitution because Thai society has advanced."**
>
> Kamnoon Sittisamarn, spokesman for the panel writing Thailand's new constitution, via Reuters. Supporters said the move would help protect transgender and gay Thai citizens.

Looks like those Thai "ladyboys" formed their own political action group.

"Don't trust any thought you have while sitting down."

~ *Friedrich Nietzsche, German philosopher*

PBI # 18: Creative Calculations

Playing around with simple calculations can sometimes provide good exercise for your brain. For example, have you ever wondered how much time a typical person spends in some ordinary activity – say, passing gas – during a lifetime?

Run the numbers: assume maybe 3–4 toots per hour, times 24 hours per day, times 30 days per month – that comes out to a lot of farting. Extend it to a year, and then maybe to 60 or 70 years, and, see how much time you get.

Just tryin' to give you some mental exercise . . .

Favorite Lame Joke # 7

Years ago, a Mexican farmer came into a dusty little Texas town, leading his burro, which was laden with a large cargo wrapped in an old blanket.

A couple of young bubbas were hanging around outside the hardware store, and they thought they'd have some fun with the little guy. Just some good-natured bubba fun, you know.

One of them called out, "Hey, Pancho! Come over here."

The Mexican guy walked in their direction, saying politely, "Yes, señor?"

"Tell me, Pancho," bubba demanded, "can you dance?"

"No, señor – sorry – I don't know how to dance."

"I'll bet you do," snarled bubba. He pulled out his six-shooter and shot into the ground, right between the Mexican guy's feet. Reflexively, and predictably, the Mexican guy jumped up and backward.

"See," declared bubba, to the amusement of his pals. "Looks like you do know how to dance."

He fired again, and again the Mexican guy jumped. Another shot – another jump. Loud laughter from the bubbas who were gathering to see the fun.

After the Mexican guy had counted six shots, he dashed over to his burro, lifted up the blanket, and pulled out a sawed-off shotgun.

All the expressions on all the faces suddenly changed.

He walked over to the shooter, pointed the shotgun at his belly-button, and said – ever so politely – "Now, señor, I have a question for *you*."

Shaking in his boots, bubba said, "Uh – what's the question?"

"Have you ever kiss a burro's bare ass?"

"Uh – no," bubba replied, "but I have always wanted to."

Which Musical Genre Never Evolves?

Of all the many different genres of music known to the Western world, only one – only one – never seems to evolve.

Which one? Christmas music. It's the same lame, crappy stuff that's been around for decades, recorded in prehistoric times by a bunch of long-dead crooners. No new artists, no new tunes, no stretching the medium, no experimental stuff, no breakaway sounds – nada, nichts, zip, zilch.

Why?

Answer: because it isn't music any more. It has morphed completely into a Pavlovian signaling system, the sole purpose of which is to trigger one very specific, highly conditioned human behavior pattern: *buying stuff.*

Americans can bet on the arrival of "The Christmas Season" on the day after the national Thanksgiving holiday. That's when the background Christmas music starts playing in just about every public place and space, particularly wherever money can be spent.

And that's why one of my favorite days of the year is the day after Christmas day, because that's when it stops.

The Great Equalizer

The rich and powerful have their advantages, to be sure.

However, there is one life experience that reduces them all to the same mundane, ordinary, pathetic level as everybody else: *a nuclear case of diarrhea.*

For those few moments, they're the peers of peasants, laborers, prisoners, vagabonds, the homeless, and the insane. There is no dignity, no power, no glory, no greatness.

It truly is the great equalizer.

Big Smoke

Question: Which tobacco company is the biggest one in the world?

Answer: The China National Tobacco Company, owned by the Chinese government.

Are they motivated to get Chinese people unhooked from cigarettes? I think they are . . . NOT!

One of the Great Philosophical Questions of Life

"Do you think skunks have souls?"

So began one of the weirder conversations I've been involved in.

The guy who came to my house to trap and remove the skunks from my back yard always seemed inclined to stop and talk, but I usually got him on his way without too much chit-chat.

One day he popped his question on me.

I thought, "This is not a conversation I really want to get into," but he went ahead anyway.

"What makes you ask that?" I replied cautiously.

Soon it became clear that he was "religious," in that icky sense of the word. As he went on about his religious musings, the topic of evolution came up, even though I had tried to head it off.

"Evolution isn't a theory," he declared, knowingly. "It's just a philosophy."

Taking the bait, I asked, "Don't you accept the idea of mutation, species variation, and natural selection?"

He wandered about in a sort of intellectual swamp, and seemed to lose his train of thought.

A few minutes before, he had told me that his wife had recently died of an infection she got in a hospital, involving the "MRSA" (*methycillin resistant staphyloccocus aureus*) bacterium.

He understood that the bacterium had genetically outmaneuvered the broad spectrum antibiotics, but somehow he couldn't make the connection with the basic concepts of evolution.

As we all sometimes do, I drew a breath, got ready to explain things to him, and then breathed out and let the matter pass.

I escorted him out to his truck and got him on his way.

It's not my mission to enlighten the willfully ignorant.

English is a Weird Language: # 1

The past tense of "speak" is "spoke." Sounds better than "speaked," I guess.

Following that pattern, the past tense versions of "creak," "freak," and "sneak" would be "croke," "froke," and "snoke," right?

Not so. They're "creaked," "freaked," and "sneaked."

For some people, "sneak" becomes "snuck."

"Snuck?" Yes, "snuck."

If that's the rule, then the past tense of "speak" would be "spuck?"

The past tense for "streak" is "struck?" No, that's the past tense for "strike."

Hmmm . . . never mind.

"We used to have actresses trying to become stars.

Now we have stars trying to become actresses."

~ *Laurence Olivier, British character actor*

Failing to Succeed – or Succeeding to Fail

Something that looks like a complete failure can turn out to be a success, often to the credit of nobody in particular.

Penicillin became one of the most useful drugs in history after the Scottish scientist Alexander Fleming, in 1928, found that airborne mold spores had killed the bacteria he was growing in a Petri dish.

Vulcanization of rubber reportedly came about in the 1840s, when the American Charles Goodyear and his colleagues accidentally spilled some ordinary gum rubber on a hot surface. It changed properties considerably, and quickly outran ordinary rubber in popularity.

Ivory Soap, "The Soap that Floats" reportedly did not float until 1878, when Harley Procter and James Gamble went off and left a batch of tallow-based soap cooking in their factory. Reportedly, the mixing process had introduced more air into the soap than they intended. They supposedly became intrigued with this "failed" product and soon began to market it for its novel characteristic. Truth be told, some historians dispute this story.

Post-It Notes, those ubiquitous little sticky-backed slips of paper, were born in the 1970s, of a marriage between a "failed" adhesive – it was too weak, but it had the interesting feature of peeling and re-sticking – and the need to flag key bits of information in large documents. The novel product, neglected by 3M Corporation for almost a decade, became hugely popular with the company's own administrative workers. It eventually leaked out into the market place and made heaps of money for the firm.

Viagra, a medication famous for treating erectile dysfunction in men (a disorder known to British women as "willy nilly"), was a failed heart medication. Researchers found it had little effect on angina and similar cardiovascular disorders, but the men in the phase-2 trials didn't want to give it back. ED was increasingly understood as a vascular disorder, in which the key blood vessels don't dilate adequately. It didn't do much for the "heart" issue, but it did wonders for the "hard" issue. Viagra became a billion-dollar product in record time.

Famous for What?

Who was Betsy Ross, and what did she do that made her famous?

Why, she sewed the first American flag for George Washington – every American knows that. That famous painting of her and George proves it.

They do indeed know it, except that it's *almost certainly not true*.

Historians are now nearly unanimous in their opinions that Betsy Ross never even met George Washington, to say nothing of having ever made a flag for him.

Apparently, the legend materialized *a century after she died*, in 1870, when Ross' grandson, William Canby, made the claim to one of the historical societies.

When you have a look at the Betsy Ross Society's website, betsyrosshouse.org, you'll read a charmingly evasive reference to her role in U.S. history. Even her most loyal fans no longer claim it's true.

Lots of people have gone down in history for what they didn't do, instead of what they actually did.

PBI # 19: The Wheel? No Big Deal

We often hear people refer to the wheel as one of the important inventions of all time. "The greatest thing since the invention of the wheel."

But think about it: what good is a wheel? What could you do with it? Stand on top of it and try to roll it along?

Actually, the truly significant invention was not the wheel, but *the axle* – or more accurately, the concept of the wheel and axle as *a system*.

This must have been a profound realization for the early humans. The wheel and axle system was probably discovered – or invented – simultaneously by many humans, but for each of them the experience of perceiving a systematic relationship between two completely different objects may have been hugely exhilarating.

They could immediately make grinding wheels, wagons and carts, waterwheels, windmills, pulleys, pottery wheels – a vast number of energy-transducing systems. From bicycle wheels to roulette wheels – they all work because of the wheel-and-axle concept.

Lots of other great inventions involve pairing up two things to make a third entity, i.e. a system: the bow and arrow; the nut and bolt; the lever and fulcrum; the lock and key; the screw and screwdriver.

But the wheel by itself? No big deal.

Late Bloomers

Not every great thinker, creator, or performer makes it big in his or her lifetime. Here are three who deserved to, but didn't.

Vincent Van Gogh, the tormented Dutch genius who painted as he wanted to paint, and refused to do commercial portraits and wall hangings for the wealthy, nevertheless influenced later generations of artists in profound ways.

Vince produced hundreds of paintings in his short and troubled life, but only sold one of them. This, even though his brother Theo was a full-time commercial art dealer in Paris.

He died poor, sad, and alone, and yet his paintings change hands today for tens of millions of dollars.

Herman Melville, who lived in America during approximately the same period as Van Gogh, wrote a grand novel – Moby-Dick – which publishers and critics declared a failure during his lifetime. It sales were less than modest. As we writers tend to say, it "sank without a ripple."

But Melville didn't kill himself, or pass his later years in agony. When his early writing career couldn't support him, he took jobs on commercial ships – which gave him the experience for the book. He died in comfortable obscurity at age 72.

Only in later years did scholars and critics examine his work more closely, and then it began to get the appreciation it deserved. Modern writers and scholars now count Moby-Dick amongst the great novels of history. Its famous opening line, "Call me Ishmael," is widely quoted, studied by aspiring writers, and often used as a jumping-off place for wry humor by wry humorists.

An epic Hollywood movie, starring Gregory Peck as the psychologically flawed Captain Ahab, memorialized the book in the American popular memory.

Robert Goddard, a self-taught amateur scientist, became obsessed with the possibilities of space travel as early as 1900, extrapolating from his early experiments with rockets on his mother's farm.

In the face of general indifference and frequent ridicule, he continued to assemble a theory of rocket-powered space flight. By the time he died in 1945 – at the same time the Germans were experimenting with missiles, but well before the beginning of the American space program – he had established most of the principles that are central to rocketry today.

Goddard gets credit for building the first liquid-fueled rocket, as well as developing the first practical gyroscopic stabilization mechanism for keeping rockets on course. Together with some of his helpers, he launched rockets to altitudes of nearly a mile, at speeds of over 500 miles per hour.

In college, he developed into a technological genius, earning a Ph.D. and teaching at several universities, including Princeton. He made significant contributions to a number of other technological fields that were emerging at the time.

Goddard never lived to see manned space flight, nor the achievement of launching rockets outside the Earth's atmosphere. However, virtually all modern scientists recognize his remarkable contributions to the foundations of space exploration.

One of NASA's key facilities is named the Goddard Space Flight Center, in Greenbelt, Maryland. A crater on the moon bears his name, as a testimonial to his genius.

In the run-up to the much-anticipated Apollo 11 landing on the moon, a news reporter asked Dr. Werner Von Braun, the refugee scientist who had directed the German V-2 rocketry program, what he would advise the first man who stepped on the moon to say. How should this landmark historical event be announced?

Von Braun replied, "He should say 'Goddard, we are here.'"

Stiff Lips Cause Trips

We often hear the expression, "keep a stiff upper lip," especially associated with the British.

But that's another idea that makes no sense when you analyze it.

When you're nervous, afraid, or extremely anxious, does your upper lip quiver? Or, does the lower one quiver?

Seems to me a person would look very strange with a quivering upper lip – sort of like a neurotic rabbit.

"Keep a stiff lower lip?" I can buy that – although, now it sounds even weirder.

"Change your thoughts and you change your world."

~ *Norman Vincent Peale*, American minister, author of *The Power of Positive Thinking*

Which Door?

Here's a situation. What would you do?

You're in a public place, like a restaurant, and you feel the call of nature. You go back to the area where the restrooms are located.

Both restrooms are small, and each only accommodates one person at a time.

The door to the restroom for your gender is locked, meaning it's occupied.

However, the restroom for the other gender is unoccupied.

You're feeling some pressure to relieve yourself very soon.

Do you:

1. Persevere until the person using "your" restroom comes out? Or,

2. Go into the restroom for the other gender?

Are you conditioned to think that men's rooms are only to be used by men, and women's rooms only by women? Does this make sense? Would you feel you were behaving illogically by choosing to be uncomfortable instead of using the vacant restroom?

If you chose option # 2, would you feel strangely guilty for violating some rule of etiquette? If you saw someone of the other gender waiting to use that restroom when you came out, would you feel guilty? Would they give you a look of disapproval? If your same-gender restroom was empty by then, couldn't they have used that?

As you can see, I love to complicate simple things . . .

These Are a Few of My Favorite Words

I've always felt the word "icky" was a good one, and very under-appreciated.

It just seems to get across an idea with a very simple sound.

When you say something is icky, don't you just tend to make a face, lift up your shoulders, hunch forward, and shiver a little bit?

Icky - how many words can give you that much fun?

I've also felt for a long time that the word "moot" was a neat one, and it ought to be used more. Somebody might say, "Do you think they'll fire the CEO?"

And you can say "It's moot – I just heard he resigned."

Moot – the more you say it, the funnier it sounds. Almost like a nonsense syllable that takes on a meaning. Imagine a rock band, with the singer screeching whatever he's on about, while the back-up singers chant something like "moot . . . moot . . . moot . . ." Kids would love it.

And, what about "gargle?" There's another good one for you. It even sounds like the sound it's describing. Open your mouth wide and say "gargle, gargle, gargle" a few times. Doesn't it sound like you're actually gargling? But don't overdo it – they might decide you should be placed in protective custody, for your own good.

Gargle is one of the favorite Irish nicknames for beer. There's an old song that says, "The gargle dims me brain."

Words are such fun . . .

Can Roaches Dematerialize?

Have you ever seen a roach in your house, run to get the bug spray, and it was gone when you got back?

You searched every nook and cranny in the place, and couldn't find it?

Or, you shot it with the spray, it dashed for the nearest hideout, say under a curtain, and when you pulled back the curtain it wasn't there?

I'm convinced the little buggers can dematerialize when they're in trouble.

That would be a good trait, from the standpoint of evolution. They'll probably outlast us.

"If all of our troubles were to be piled upon a common heap
and each of us was required to take an equal portion,
most of us would be content to take our own and depart."
~ *Plato, Greek philosopher*

Lao Tzu Told Me About the Future (or the Past)

The Chinese philosopher Lao Tzu said,

"What is is the was of what will be."

I still haven't figured that out.

"The man with the best job in the country is the Vice President.
All he has to do is get up every morning and say, 'How's the
President?'"

~ *Will Rogers, American humorist*

PBI # 20: Will Cell Phones Go the Way of Cigarettes?

Years ago, smokers in the U.S. and many other countries typically
felt completely free to light up anywhere they liked, even though
they were outnumbered two to one by those who didn't smoke.
Non-smokers suffered in silence, usually feeling that it wasn't
worth making a scene while someone else was fouling the air they
had to breathe.

Eventually, it became customary to divide restaurants, airplanes,
trains, buses, meeting rooms, and other public spaces into smoking
and non-smoking sections.

Finally, the 40 percent of Americans who were addicted to that
socially acceptable drug habit gradually got pushed into a corner –
literally and figuratively – and many public spaces finally
eliminated smoking altogether. Once smokers were on the run, the
courageous news media piled on and finished them off. Smokers in
the U.S. today account for only about 22 percent of the population.

We'll probably come to the point where the public space gets
divided again, with 25% allocated to those addicted to cell phones,
and the rest of the space cell-phone free.

Today, cell phone addicts seem to feel the same sense of privilege
in the acoustic environment, completely oblivious to the dirty
looks from those around them. But eventually, the social pressure
forced smokers into a defensive position, and their pleas that their
civil rights were being violated didn't sell. It seems pretty likely
that cell phone addicts are heading for the same destiny.

One of my favorite restaurants is in a club patronized mostly by
hard-charging business people, and it has a firm policy: *no cell
phones in the dining room.*

I'm looking forward to the day . . .

Persistent? Or Pig-Headed?

Part of intellectual courage is knowing when to take advice from others and when to trust your own judgments. Let's compare two famous people from history who followed their convictions.

Let's consider case #1:

Some time during the period around 200 BC, a famous general named Hannibal, who fought for the North African empire of Carthage, launched a ferocious attack against the Roman army in the African desert at a place called Zama.

Hannibal employed a novel weapon in his attack: elephants. He had become a big fan of elephants as instruments of war. They were huge, frightening beasts, and enemy soldiers were usually intimidated by their mere presence. His father, Hamilcar, had experimented with elephants – mostly without success – and Hannibal himself had led an army equipped with elephants across the Italian Alps to attack the farther reaches of the early Roman empire. The fact that he lost half of his army and most of the elephants on the way did nothing to dampen his enthusiasm for this military innovation.

Hannibal, his soldiers, and his elephants confronted the famous Roman general Scipio, who commanded a force of about an equal number of soldiers. Hannibal was utterly convinced that the elephants would give him the decisive advantage.

The battle began with a massive frontal assault, with Hannibal's soldiers following more than 100 mounted elephants charging across the whole width of Scipio's infantry line. Scipio, however, was known as a clever general who could think up strategies and tactics to suit the unique situations he encountered. He had worked out a simple method for dealing with the elephants.

As the charge developed, Scipio's army reformed, opening large alleys into which they redirected the charging elephants. Rather than attacking the elephants, they killed their drivers, rendering

153

the elephants uncontrollable and useless in the battle. By shouting and banging their swords against their shields, Scipio's soldiers raised an enormous din that frightened the elephants. The riderless elephants, now completely out of control and terrified, turned and stampeded, trampling hundreds of Hannibal's soldiers. Scipio had turned Hannibal's elephants into weapons against him.

The battle turned into a complete rout and Hannibal was so utterly defeated that he advised the rulers of Carthage to surrender, ending the Second Punic War.

Yet, curiously, even though the elephants had been a colossal failure in almost every campaign, Hannibal – even to his deathbed – never admitted it. "If I had only had more elephants," he insisted, "I could have defeated them."

Now, let's consider case #2:

Guglielmo Marconi, an Italian inventor and one of the early pioneers of radio and electronics, believed that it was possible to send radio signals over long distances, so that people would be able to communicate between continents.

The weight of almost all reputable scientific opinion stood against him. Scientists in 1900 believed that radio waves, which traveled in straight lines, could never be used over long distances because of the limitations imposed by the curvature of the earth.

Marconi decided to try it anyway.

On December 12, 1901, he set up a specially designed wireless receiver in Newfoundland, Canada, and received a Morse-code signal – the letter "S," represented by three pulses, or "dots" – from Poldhu, Cornwall, in England.

Just over a year later, on Jan. 18, 1903, he sent a message of greetings from President Theodore Roosevelt to King Edward VII, who sent his reply.

Several years later, scientists discovered the *ionosphere*, the layer of charged particles in the earth's atmosphere that have the effect of *refracting*, or "bending" short-wave radio signals, causing them to follow the contours of the earth. Marconi's persistence paid off: he received the Nobel Prize in physics in 1909.

Maybe Hannibal and Marconi both have lessons to teach us. "Hannibal-ism" is the drive to persist in an unsuccessful course of

154

action, in the face of evidence that it's not working. "Marconi-ism" is the courage to persist when there's no evidence to go on. Both men probably deserve credit for ignoring the advice of those around them, but the fatal mistake is *ignoring the evidence* when it's clear.

Still, when you undertake any big adventure – especially against the advice of your peers – it might help to ask yourself, "Is this a Hannibal venture, or a Marconi venture?" The answer, unfortunately, isn't always clear.

Dopey Definitions # 3

Carcinoma, n. A valley in California, notable for its heavy smog.

Circumvent, n. The opening in the front of boxer shorts.

Conflagration, n. A reporter's first fire.

Destinesia, n. The act of going into a room and forgetting why.

Lymph, v. To walk with a lithp.

Rectitude, n. The formal, dignified demeanor assumed by a proctologist immediately before he examines you.

Pollymorph, n. A mutated parrot.

Dilate, n. To live a long life.

Subdued, n. A guy who, like, works on one of those, like, submarines.

Willy-nilly, n. Erectile dysfunction.

Factoids # 5

❖ Multiply 111,111,111 by itself and you get a surprisingly symmetrical number. Try it on your calculator.

❖ Some hospitals salvage the umbilical cords of newborn babies. The tough, fibrous tissues work extremely well for vein transplant surgery.

❖ The city of Reno, Nevada is west of Los Angeles, California. The city of Detroit is east of Tallahassee, Florida. The highest point in Pennsylvania is lower than the lowest point in Colorado.

❖ The longest recorded flight of a chicken is claimed to be thirteen seconds. I haven't verified this; I wasn't present at the time. (I imagine the chicken was trying to escape the executioner.)

❖ The phrase "rule of thumb" supposedly came from an old English law that prohibited a man from beating his wife with a stick wider than his thumb.

❖ The term "the whole nine yards" reportedly arose with WWII aerial gunners in the Pacific. They loaded their airplanes with .50 caliber machine gun belts measuring 27 feet. If a gunner fired an entire ammo belt at a target, he gave it "the whole nine yards."

❖ The microwave oven arrived when an engineer walked by a radar apparatus in a laboratory, and discovered that a chocolate bar in his pocket was melting. The *magnetron* tube, developed toward the end of WWII, generated powerful electromagnetic emissions used for radar transmitters. Percy LeBaron Spencer, of the Raytheon Company, reportedly determined that certain frequencies of radio energy could excite water molecules to high energy levels, and thereby cook just about any food that might have a significant water content. That led to the Radar Range, the first commercial microwave oven.

Pronounce Your Words Clearly

Person A: "Use the word "hominy" in a sentence."

Person B: "Hominy times do I have to tell you to close the door when you come in?"

"I want to love you without clutching,
appreciate you without judging,
join you without invading,
invite you without demanding,
leave you without guilt,
criticize you without blaming,
and help you without insulting.
If I can have the same from you
then we can truly meet and enrich each other."
~ *Virginia Satir, American therapist, pioneer of family therapy*

You Could Get Hooked on Grooks

Piet Hein, one of Denmark's leading screwball thinkers, invented "Grooks," which are short verses about weird aspects of life.

Examples:

Life: "I'd like to know what this whole show is all about, before it's out."

Understanding: "I sometimes think that reality is like two locked boxes, each one holding the other one's key."

Patience: "Put up in a place where it's easy to see, this cryptic admonishment: TTT. When you think how discouragingly slowly you climb, it's well to remember that Things Take Time."

Assignment: try writing a couple of grooks of your own.

Look up: *Grooks* by Piet Hein

Can Anybody Be President?

You can run for President of the U.S. if you like, but don't expect to win unless you look, walk, and talk like a lot like the presidents of the past.

For example, no American president has ever had a surname that was difficult to pronounce. Think about it: Washington, Adams,

Jefferson, Lincoln, Wilson, Clinton, Bush, Obama. The only ones with slightly weird names were Roosevelt (two of 'em), and maybe Eisenhower. A president named Tsongas? Dukakis? Wocziejowicz? Probably not gonna happen.

Young guys these days like the half-beard look – you know, the one where they look like they've just come off of a three-day drunk and haven't had a bath. But beards have never been popular with U.S. presidents.

Look at the official presidential portraits. The first 15 guys did not have beards or mustaches. Lincoln was the first president with a beard, and he apparently started a trend for a while. Eight out of the ten presidents who followed him had beards.

Then the beards went out of style. No president in the last 100 years, starting with Woodrow Wilson, has had a beard.

As of this writing, Americans have elected only one non-white president – Barack Obama. A female president might also be a significant break from the pattern, especially considering that women got the right to vote less than 100 years ago.

Favorite lame Joke # 8

A woman went to visit the local psychic, with the hope of contacting her dearly departed grandmother. The psychic went into a trance, her eyelids began to flutter, and she began to moan softly.

Eventually, a voice was heard, "Granddaughter? Are you there?"

The granddaughter, wide-eyed, responded, "Grandma? Is that you?"

"Yes granddaughter, it's me."

"It's really you, Grandma?" the woman repeated, astonished.

"Yes, it's really me, granddaughter. What do you want to know?"

The woman paused a moment. "Grandma, I have just one question for you."

"Yes, my child," intoned the voice. "Anything."

"When did you learn to speak English?"

"To make a great dream come true,

you must first have a great dream."

~ *Hans Selye, physician, father of the medical concept of stress*

✪ ✪ ✪ ✪ ✪

The (Only) Five Basic Fears We All Live By

President Franklin Roosevelt famously asserted, "The only thing we have to *feah*, is *feah* itself." I think he was right, actually.

Fear of fear probably causes more problems in our lives than fear. That claim needs a bit of explaining, I know.

Fear seems to have gotten a bad rap amongst most human beings. And it's not nearly as complicated as we try to make it.

A simple and useful definition of fear is:

> An anxious feeling, caused by our anticipation
> of some imagined event or experience.

Medical experts tell us that the anxious feeling we get when we're afraid is a standardized biological reaction. It's pretty much the same set of body signals, whether we're afraid of getting bitten by a dog, getting turned down for a date, or getting our taxes audited.

Fear, like all other emotions, is basically *information*. It offers us knowledge and understanding – if we choose to accept it – of our psychobiological status.

There are only five basic fears, out of which almost all of our other so-called fears are manufactured. Those five basic fears are:

- ❖ *Extinction* – fear of annihilation, of ceasing to exist. This is a more fundamental way to express it than just calling it the "fear of death". The idea of *no longer being* arouses a primal *existential anxiety* in all normal humans. Consider that panicky feeling you get when you look over the edge of a high building.

- ❖ *Mutilation* – fear of losing any part of our precious bodily structure; the thought of having our body's boundaries invaded, or of losing the integrity of any organ, body part, or natural function. For example, anxiety about animals, such as bugs, spiders, snakes, and other creepy things arises from fear of mutilation.

❖ *Loss of Autonomy* – fear of being immobilized, paralyzed, restricted, enveloped, overwhelmed, entrapped, imprisoned, smothered, or controlled by circumstances. In a physical form, it's sometimes known as claustrophobia, but it also extends to social interactions and relationships.

❖ *Separation* – fear of abandonment, rejection, and loss of connectedness – of *becoming a non-person* – not wanted, respected, or valued by anyone else. The "silent treatment," when imposed by a group, can have a devastating psychological effect on the targeted person.

❖ *Ego-death* – fear of humiliation, shame, or any other mechanism of *profound self-disapproval* that threatens the loss of integrity of the Self; fear of the shattering or disintegration of one's constructed sense of lovability, capability, and worthiness.

That's all – just those five. You can think of them as forming a simple hierarchy – call it the "feararchy."

Think about the various common labels we put on our fears. Start with the easy ones: fear of heights or falling is basically fear of extinction (possibly accompanied by significant mutilation, but that's sort of secondary).

Fear of failure? Read it as fear of ego-death.

Fear of rejection? It's fear of separation, and probably also fear of ego-death. The terror many people have at the idea of having to speak in public is basically fear of ego-death.

Fear of intimacy, or "fear of commitment" is basically fear of losing one's autonomy.

Some other emotions we know by various popular names are also expressions of these primary fears. If you track them down to their most basic levels, the basic fears show through.

Jealousy, for example, is an expression of the fear of separation, or devaluation: "She'll value him more than she values me." At the extreme, it can express the fear of ego-death: "I'll be a worthless person." Envy works the same way.

160

Shame and guilt express the fear – or the actual condition – of separation and even ego-death. The same is true for embarrassment and humiliation.

Fear is often the base emotion on which anger floats. Oppressed peoples rage against their oppressors because they fear – or actually experience – loss of autonomy and even ego-death. The destruction of a culture or a religion by an invading occupier may be experienced as a kind of collective ego-death. Those who make us fearful will also make us angry.

Religious bigotry and intolerance may express the fear of ego-death on a cosmic level, and can even extend to existential anxiety. "If my god isn't the right god, or the best god, then I'll be stuck without a god. Without god on my side, I'll be at the mercy of the impersonal forces of the environment. My ticket could be canceled at any moment, without a reason."

Some of our fears, of course, have basic survival value. Others, however, are learned reflexes that can be weakened or re-learned.

That strange idea of "fearing our fears" can become less strange when we realize that many of our avoidance reactions – turning down an invitation to a party if we tend to feel uncomfortable in groups; putting off the doctor's appointment; or not asking for the raise – are instant reflexes that are reactions to the memories of fear.

They happen so quickly that we don't actually experience the full effect of the fear. We experience a "micro-fear" – a reaction that's a kind of shorthand code for the real fear. This reflex reaction has the same effect of causing us to evade and avoid as the real fear. This is why it's fairly accurate to say that many of our so-called fear reactions are actually the fears of fears.

When we let go of our notion of fear as the welling up of evil forces within us – the Freudian motif – and begin to see fear and its companion emotions as basically *information*, we can think about them consciously. And the more clearly and calmly we can articulate the origins of the fear, the less our fears frighten us and control us.

Why Don't We Have Women "Juniors?"

The custom of giving male children the same first names as their fathers has been around for a long time in Western societies.

Two pairs of U.S. presidents – the Adams's and the Bushes, were "senior" and "junior" versions. When people speak of "John F. Kennedy Jr.," they invoke the long shadow of the charismatic martyred president as they refer to his son.

Yet it's exceedingly rare for a woman to bear the same first name as her mother. To refer to someone as "Mary Jones, Jr." – even before she marries and possibly gives up her family name – would sound so strange as to seem somehow socially unacceptable.

The question seems to be one that conjures up all sorts of determined attempts to "make sense" of society, to "explain" why things are the way they are. And yet it might just be one of those unanswerable ones: that's just the way it is.

PBI # 21: How About Organized Shoot-Outs?

Just about every week, somewhere in the U.S., some berserker decides to shoot a bunch of people and – usually – get killed in the process. That seems very inconsiderate to the people who get killed. Even if they knew the shooter well and even tormented him, it's going to extremes.

People who don't get along with one another rarely shoot one another, so why should a few individuals be allowed to stage a massacre? If they want to kill somebody and get killed in the process, they could just as easily kill one another – we'd just have to organize it for them.

Picture the scene: a large open area, maybe a stadium parking lot or some similar place where swap meets, or concerts, or sporting events usually take place. Maybe the stadium itself. A crowd of people would gather on a Saturday, and buy tickets to watch. The organizers would set up trees, barriers, and various other obstacles to hide behind, and the protagonists could stalk one another.

They'd have signed up in advance, and they'd all get similar weapons. People could root for their favorite maniacs, and they could place bets on who'd get killed when. Businesses could buy advertising space on the backs of the shooters' jackets; the shooters wouldn't have to pay for anything.

A huge scoreboard, video screens, an announcer – of course, it would all be televised. Scenes of the protagonists stalking one another; close-up views of kill shots; the dying words of some of the losers – it would all make great TV. Advertising revenues might beat the Super Bowl.

When they got down to the last man, the audience would decide, by thumbs up or thumbs down, whether he could go free. Thumbs down, and he gets the choice of either shooting himself, or dying in a shoot-out with cops (who would, of course get extra pay).

Too shocking, too brutal, you say? Oh, come on – it has all the ingredients of our most popular forms of entertainment, packaged up neatly. There's something in it for everybody. It's the American Way of doing things.

An Easy Way to Save the Postal Service

I don't know why so many people are agonizing about how to save the U.S. Postal Service. Ben Franklin started it, and it's been a permanent part of American society for over 200 years. Times have changed, and it's losing money again, so it has to change with the times.

The solution is easy if you think about it a bit.

Instead of adding a paltry few cents to the price of a first-class stamp, let's increase the price to where it really belongs: a dollar – just like most lottery tickets. Every stamp can have a serial number printed on it, and the stamp will become a lottery ticket.

Problem solved.

Nitwitticisms # 4

"The police are not there to create disorder. They're there to *maintain* disorder."
~ *Mayor Frank Daley of Chicago*

Television interviewer: "I understand that when you were young, you were asthmatic."
"I beg your pardon! I've always been Catholic."

~ Philippine Vice President (later President) Joseph Estrada

"Mr. Nixon was the thirty-seventh President of the United States. He had been preceded by thirty-six others."
~ U.S. President Gerald Ford

"A low voter turnout is an indication of fewer people going to the polls."
~ U.S. President George W. Bush

"The Kabbalah helps you confront your fears. Like, if a girl borrowed my clothes and never gave them back, and I saw her wearing them months later, I would confront her."
~ Socialite Paris Hilton, explaining the benefits of studying the Kabbalah

"That's Hendrick's 19th home run. One more and he reaches double figures."
~ Sportscaster Jerry Coleman

"You read what Disraeli had to say. I don't remember what he said. He said something. He's no longer with us."
~ U.S Senator Bob Dole, commenting on the Clinton-Lewinsky sex scandal

Have the Brits Lost Their Boobs?

5h	Monday's issue of The Sun was missing one familiar feature: **a topless model on Page 3.** The Guardian says the British tabloid has ended the practice after 44 years.
	The Associated Press ↗

"There is a tide in the affairs of men
Which, taken at the flood, leads on to fortune;
Omitted, all the voyage of their life
Is bound in shallows and in miseries.
On such a full sea are we now afloat,
And we must take the current when it serves,
Or lose our venture."
~ *Brutus, in "Julius Caesar," Act 4, Scene 3*

Choose Your Own Handle?

Research shows that as many as seventeen percent of adults don't like their first name, and wish they had a different one (OK, I made that up – but I bet it's close).

You might like your own name, but how would you like to carry around a handle like:

- o   Batman (OK in Singapore, but not in the U.S.);
- o   Joker (OK in the Philippines, not in the U.S.);
- o   Edsel (OK for a car – or maybe not – but not for a person);
- o   Moon Unit (inflicted by a weird show-business couple);
- o   Whoopi (she copes, I presume).
- o   King Lear (a guy I worked with years ago).
- o   Morgan Death (another guy I worked with).

As always, my solution is simple and easy. The name they give you when you're born serves as a temporary handle, and it legally expires on your eighteenth birthday. On that day, you have to choose a permanent name and file it with the government. You can keep your temporary name, or take up any one you like.

It would be a great excuse for a party . . .

Take it One Step at a Time

Some of life's problems get simpler and easier if you break them down into parts, and solve them one step at a time. Here's a good exercise for warming up your logic muscles – the "word ladder."

The idea is to start with one word, and by changing only one letter at a time, transform it into another word, with the restriction that every change of a letter creates another valid word.

Punctuations are allowed. Here's an example:

Change "came" to "went:"

> came => ca[n]e
>
> cane => can['t]
>
> can't => [w]ant
>
> want =>w[e]nt

Here are some others to practice on.

Change hate to love

Change fall to rise

Change take to give

Change lose to find

Change won't to will

The Ancient Greeks Would Have Loved McDonald's

Historians tell us that the Roman Empire began its rise to glory at roughly the same time that classic Greek culture was declining – give or take a century or so. The Greeks were consummate architects and sculptors, but the Romans became consummate engineers. Curiously, the ancient Greeks never figured out the *arch* – the absolutely fundamental feature of almost all Roman structures, and later the defining feature of Gothic cathedral building.

As a result, Greek buildings had to have lots of columns. Think, for example, of the famous *Parthenon*, the temple to Athena, patron goddess of Athens. The maximum possible distance between any

166

two columns was restricted by the strength of the horizontal stone beams parked on top of them. All types of stone are very strong in compression, but relatively weak in tension, or bending. Roman arch-based structures, such as the famous aqueducts in Segovia, Spain, still stand after nearly 2,000 years.

Perhaps even more curiously, the Incas of Peru didn't invent the arch, either, even though experts rate them as some of the most skilled stone masons in history. Up until the time of their fall at the hands of Francisco Pizarro in the sixteenth century, they still built narrow doorways, hallways, and chambers with post and beam designs.

"Denunciation of the young

is a necessary part of the hygiene of older people,

and greatly assists in the circulation of their blood."

~ *Logan Pearsall Smith, American humorist*

You Can't Win

Comedian Richard Lewis, known for his preoccupation with mental stress, says:

"You can't win with the shrinks.

If you're late for your appointment, he'll say you're resisting therapy.

But if you get there early, he'll say you're anxious.

What if you get there exactly on time? Then he says you're compulsive."

Don't Mess With Shakespeare

I herewith register a formal complaint: I demand that theater people cease and desist – immediately – from trying to "modernize," or "improve," Shakespeare's plays with their own cute little invented gimmicks.

Imagine paying your thirty bucks to see what's advertised as one of Bill's 37 blockbuster plays, and then having to sit there in the audience as King Lear comes on stage in a wheelchair.

Or watching Shylock appear on stage dressed in a pinstriped suit.

Or seeing an ostentatiously gay character in a newly minted scene, which seems to have no relevance to the rest of "Midsummer Night's Dream."

It ain't right.

I don't know why I've allowed it continue as long as I have.

What the Amish Can Teach Us About Technology

Pediatricians in the U.S. have started warning us, emphatically, about the effects of television, video games, and other electronic media on the cognitive and social development of American children. The American Academy of Pediatrics strongly recommends that no child under the age of two be exposed to *screen-based media of any kind*. They recommend that teens should not spend more than *two hours per day* with entertainment media – as contrasted to the current American average of about seven hours.

Parents and mental health experts increasingly lament the addictive effects of social media and online games on teen-agers.

Police and public officials are alarmed by the increasing incidence of gun-wielding berserkers, and the possibility that sensationalized media coverage might be causing it.

Some citizens are increasingly anxious about the loss of personal privacy and identity, intrusive commercialism, hedonistic values, and government surveillance without legal cause.

But in the inner circles of techno-America, not many people seem all that concerned.

Are we helpless to stop or redirect the relentless invasion of electronic media – "technology," as it's popularly known – into our lives?

Are we witnessing the disintegration or destruction of the American culture as we've known it? Does it matter to anybody?

Maybe we should ask the Amish for advice.

The Amish in America – and their counterparts, the Mennonites – are a culture within a culture, with very distinct boundaries separating them from the majority "exo-culture." Few people in the majority culture have more than a superficial understanding of the way the Amish culture works.

Here are some reasons why the Amish might be better qualified than most "experts" to advise the members of the majority culture on the impact of technology and the need to manage and control it.

Amish communities in the U.S., especially the large ones in Pennsylvania, Ohio, and Indiana, are as strong, cohesive, and self-managing as they've ever been. Contrary to popular belief, their numbers are not declining, but are growing steadily, driven by the combination of large families and impressively high retention rates – typically 80–85%. This is true worldwide.

The best way to understand the Amish culture is to focus on what they want, not what they don't want. Amish typically don't completely reject popular culture, commercialism, and technology because they consider them "sinful." Their policy is more accurately understood as one of *selective adoption*, with very high thresholds of acceptance.

Some Amish communities use no electricity; others do. Power tools are acceptable in some situations and not in others. Few Amish people own cars, but some of them willingly ride in cars. Few of them use cell phones, but some do. Televisions are rare, but not non-existent.

Decisions to adopt or reject various features of the outer culture are typically managed consciously and carefully. Certain elders of each Amish community are empowered to set policy, and typically all the heads of families who are part of the same quasi-clan structure accept and apply those policies. Over time, each important element of the surrounding culture gets careful scrutiny. Members discuss its potential benefits to the community, as well as its perceived impacts on the Amish way of life. Each option is adjudicated as in, or out, or sometimes placed on well-scrutinized "probation." In almost all cases, the elders decide its fate based on a kind of cost-benefit reasoning process.

Two powerful, over-arching, uncompromising priorities guide the entire Amish philosophy of selective adoption. The first is the preservation and enforcement of *devout religious practice* amongst all members of the community – with no exceptions. The second is the preservation and enforcement of their *core values* of community and collectivism – allegiance to family and clan;

cooperation and sharing of resources; humility; simplicity; thrift; contemplation; compliance with cultural norms; and obedience to the authority of the (male) elders.

Any new idea, invention, commercial product, or social practice that, on balance, seems to undermine the fabric of religious practice or erode the social order gets a thumbs-down. If its potential benefits outweigh its side effects, it may get adopted.

Amish young people, when they get to about 16–18 years old, have the option of: 1) leaving the community; or 2) permanently dedicating themselves to fully compliant membership. They are typically allowed to experiment with worldly practices for a couple of years: riding in cars, going to movies, going to parties, using cell phones, and visiting the big cities. By age 18, they must make their choice. There's no cafeteria option; it's all in, or all out.

Granted, the practices just described are so far removed from the mainstream practices of the wider American culture that there's little risk of the Amish model taking over. But, do their core doctrines make sense in some way, particularly to those in the outer culture who are increasingly concerned about the unmanaged impacts of the commercial-electronic environment?

It wouldn't be easy to apply the Amish method. The American culture has no process for vetting the fruits and consequences of the techno-media tidal wave. It's all determined by the producers, the advertisers, and the marketplace. Americans are compliant consumers, even eager consumers. And they freely allow just about any business or any celebrity to sell just about anything to their children.

By contrast to the Amish, there are no "elders" of the American culture. There is no clan structure to promote and reinforce key values. There is no code – no *Ordnung*, as the German progenitors of the Amish laid it out. Indeed, there is no "culture," in the same sense that the Amish recognize, define, cherish, and preserve their culture. There is only the "culture of now" that is evolving explosively in the media saturated commercial environment.

Could we, should we, set a new standard of scrutiny for the rapidly spreading techno-media culture? If so, who might do it, and how? This might be a new role for existing religious institutions. Or, secular advocacy organizations might emerge to take on the challenge.

By the time we fully understand where the techno-media culture is taking us, there will be no coming back.

Don't Mess With Geezers

Sign over a cubicle in a small manufacturing company:

> Age and treachery
> Will triumph over
> Youth and skill.

H.L. Mencken: the American Curmudgeon

Henry Louis "H.L." Mencken, a newspaperman from the early days of the *Baltimore Sun*, liked to express himself succinctly. And, many of his contemporaries, might add, cynically. Consider a few choice examples of his view of society.

- o "Don't overestimate the decency of the human race."
- o "The cynics are right nine times out of ten."
- o "Historians are failed novelists."
- o "The ideal client is a frightened millionaire."
- o "The first efficiency expert was Simon Legree."
- o "The great secret to happiness in love is to be glad the other fellow married her."
- o "Nobody ever went broke underestimating the taste of the American public."

PBI # 22: Throw the Bastard Out?

Presidential elections in the U.S. are extremely disruptive, and the political process becomes especially destructive when the occupant of the White House – and his political party – are trying to hang on for a second term. The country goes into an emotional tizzy while the two big power factions – having had three years to build up their war machines – figuratively fight to the death.

Very little of significance gets accomplished by Congress or the White House during the year of the second election. Journalism degenerates to the level of a rugby match, and there's little room in the electronic culture for the ideas and issues that really count.

To make things worse, the uproar and confusion caused by the hand-over – firing and hiring cabinet members; purging the top ranks of the various government agencies; vacating and moving into offices – tend to paralyze the government for at least six months or more.

There's a better way: we can replace the traditional four-year presidential term, and its optional second installment, with a single six-year term. One shot – that's it. Make your mark and you're out the door.

This is not a new idea; it's been circulating for some time. It would require a constitutional amendment – something rarely done in modern times. All of the living ex-presidents favor changing to a single six-year term.

But curiously, the American press seems to show little interest in it. Maybe they anticipate that politics wouldn't be as much fun to report on?

How Do You Define Success?

Our definitions of success seem to shift as we get older.

- o At age 4, success is not peeing in your pants.
- o At age 12, success is having friends.
- o At age 16, success is having your driver's license.
- o At age 20, success is having sex.
- o At age 35, success is having money.
- o At age 50, success is having money.
- o At age 60, success is having sex.
- o At age 70, success is having your driver's license.
- o At age 75, success is having friends.
- o At age 80, success is not peeing in your pants.

Is There a Pill for "Dumb?"

Q: What's the last thing a redneck says before he wakes up in the Emergency Department?

A: "Hey! Watch this!"

According to news reports, two good ol' boys went ice fishing out on a large lake, somewhere in the Midwest.

Not wanting to go to the trouble of carving an access hole through the ice, they decided on a short cut: dynamite.

The "brains" of the pair, who swore he had done this before, got out a stick of dynamite, attached a blasting cap and fuse, lit the fuse, and threw it out onto the ice.

Can you say "unintended consequences?" Their loyal dog, taking the thrown stick as an invitation to play, ran after it.

He picked up the dynamite stick in his mouth and dashed back toward them, probably hoping to give it back and maybe fetch it again.

The bubbas, stricken with fright, began throwing every loose object they could find at the dog, hoping to scare him off. Presumably, they were resigned to losing the dog to a terrible fate.

The dog, however, confused by this sudden expression of disapproval, ran and hid under their SUV, which was parked on the ice.

You can probably guess how it turned out: the dynamite detonated, killing the unfortunate dog, and blasting a hole in the ice bigger than the SUV.

They stood in stunned silence as the SUV bubbled below the surface, settling on the bottom of the lake.

"The biggest obstacle to learning something new
is the belief that you already know it."

~ *Shunryu Suzuki, Zen master*

173

Raining Fish?

For the past century or so, people living in the city of Yoro, Honduras, have reported heavy rains during which they claim blind fish fall from the sky.

The strange annual occurrence, known as "lluvia de peces," has defied explanation for years, and natives prefer their own religious interpretations to the more mundane ones offered by scientists.

One theory holds that the fish may have been whirled up by giant waterspouts during the rainstorms, transported across land, and deposited as the twisters died out. This, however, would qualify as a remarkably repeatable weather phenomenon.

Uncorroborated reports of a scientific expedition to Yoro suggest that the fish – all belonging to the same blind freshwater species – were living in underground streams, and surfaced as they flooded from the rains. However, no one has claimed to know where the streams open to the surface.

The favorite explanation among the locals, understandably, is that God is answering the prayers of one of their favorite patrons, Father Jose Subirana, who put in his request for divinely provided food some time in the 1800s.

"You gave your life to become the person you are right now. Was it worth it?"

~ Henry David Thoreau, American philosopher and writer

Are You a Control Freak? Take This Quiz and Find Out

Psychologists tell us about the "strength-weakness paradox," which means that any trait that's one of your best strengths can turn into a liability or a weakness if over-deployed.

Being diligent and persistent, for example, can be great but can turn into bull-headedness when taken to extremes. Open-mindedness and willingness to consider all points of view can be great, and it can also make you wishy-washy if you overdo it.

Being well-organized and getting things done can be great, but overdo it and you start acting like a "control freak." If you're a super-organized, decisive, action person, is it possible you've taken it too far? Could you be a control freak?

Control freaks, according to psychologists, come in two basic flavors, with some people showing signs of both. One type has a pervading, unconscious fear of loss of control – they get anxious and reactive in situations that are confused or unpredictable. They have a low *tolerance for ambiguity*.

The other type is motivated by unconscious power needs – they've become almost addicted to the feelings of proving themselves, being in charge, and getting their way.

In other words, some control freaks are driven to control their environments, some are driven to control the people around them, and some crave both.

This little quiz, although not scientifically perfect and probably not psychologically complete, can give you a quick perspective on your own control-seeking tendencies.

For each question, choose a number on a five-point scale, to show how accurately you think the statement describes you. Use:

1 = Rarely or Never;
2 = Seldom;
3 = Sometimes;
4 = Often; and
5 = Very Often.

Then add up all ten scores and consult the interpretation scale at the end. (Note: the even-numbered questions indicate personal control and the odd-numbered ones indicate control over others.)

Be as honest as you can. As you answer each question, imagine that someone who knows you well is looking over your shoulder – what would they say? Would they agree with your self-perception?

The Control Freak Quiz

1. Do you "help" other people drive – tell them what route to take, when to turn, where to park, remind them that the traffic light has changed?

2. Do you devote a lot of attention and energy to keeping your personal environment organized?

3. Do you give people a lot of "shoulds" and "oughts" – unsolicited advice, suggestions, and "constructive criticism?"

4. Do you have lots of personal rules, routines, rituals, and ceremonies?

5. Are you the one who takes over and orders other people around when the situation seems confused?

6. Do you dislike depending on others, accepting help from them, or allowing them to do things for you?

7. Do you insist on "being right," having things done your way, or having the final word?

8. Do you "over-plan" simple activities?

9. Do you find it difficult to admit making mistakes, being wrong or misinformed about something, or acknowledging that you've changed your mind?

10. Do you become angry, irritable, or anxious when someone or something makes you late, when things don't start on time, or things don't go according to plan?

Now Interpret Your Score:

41 – 50: yep, you're a control freak.

31 – 40: you probably have some control issues.

21 – 30: you can live and let live.

10 – 20: are you being honest?

The American "SouperBowl"

Americans spend a phenomenal amount of money on commercial sports. Probably their all-time favorite sports event is the Super Bowl, the annual clash of the National Football League's top teams – always held on a Sunday.

While fifty or so of the world's toughest athletes compete on the gridiron, millions of overweight, out-of-shape bubbas chow down on fattening food and drink lots of beer.

How much food and beer, you ask?

The National Retail Federation, which tracks spending patterns daily and hourly, estimates that on this one day, Americans spend $12 billion on food, drink, game-themed merchandise, and electronics. They buy over 7 million new TV sets just for "game day."

They eat 1.2 billion pounds of fried chicken wings; 79 million pounds of guacamole and 11 million pounds of chips; 32 million slices of pizza; and 50 million cases of beer.

On Monday, 7 million of them call in sick, and antacid sales jump by 20 percent.

Many police officers swear that the crime rate across the country drops significantly during that special 4-hour stretch.

"Not all who wander are lost."

~ J.R.R. (John Ronald Ruel) Tolkien, British writer of fantasy fiction

What's In That Bag?

While riding on a plane between Sydney and Canberra some years ago, I noticed a brightly colored paper bag, folded and neatly tucked into the seat pocket in front of me.

I pulled it out to have a look at it.

It turned out to be a film mailer – a bag into which you could put your exposed roll of film, together with some cash, and inscribe your address. The good people who provided the bag promised to develop my film and mail the photos to me within a few short days.

Then I noticed something else unusual about the bag. The message on the flip side explained that, if I should happen to become nauseated while on the flight, I was welcome to use it as a barf bag.

That struck me as rather clever – a dual-purpose product, although the two purposes seemed rather strangely incompatible.

Then I had another thought, a rather frightening one:

If I were an employee working in the film processing lab, whenever I opened one of those bags, I'd sure be hoping that the person who mailed it understood the instructions fully.

PBI # 23: Get Out an' Vote!

Australia is one of a few countries that have solved the problem of voter apathy and low turnout. They don't have to worry about whether one political party is pandering to a particular self-interested segment of the population, or whether a skewed voter response could favor one political agenda over another.

For at least three decades, voter turnout in Australian national elections has never fallen below 90 percent, and usually averages about 95 percent.

How do they do it? Simple – *voting is mandatory*. If you don't vote, you have to pay a fine. The fine isn't very high, but it has helped to establish a nationwide habit pattern: everybody has to vote.

Think of what this would mean: an indisputably *accurate measure of citizen preference*. Gone would be all worries about whether any particular ethnic, social, or economic sub-group "stays home," or is over-represented. How could a candidate ride into office on the vote of a particular special-interest cohort, when there are so many of them to be pandered to?

Suppose this system were adopted in America: how might the political process be different?

Is "A Ton" a Lot?

When my first book came out, many years ago, one of my close friends congratulated me, saying, "I hope you sell a ton of 'em."

I was pleased by his good wishes, but I later began to wonder, "How many books are there in a ton?"

I put a book on a scale and found it weighed about one pound.

At a pound per book, a ton of books would only be about 2,000 copies – a long, long way from best-sellerdom.

I discovered that the typical nonfiction book in the U.S. sells about 5,000 copies in its lifetime, and that about half of the books published don't sell enough copies to cover their costs.

So, if your book doesn't sell at least 2-1/2 tons, your editor's kids might not go to college.

"The proper office of a friend is to stick by you when you're in the wrong.

Nearly anybody will stick by you when you're in the right."

~ *Mark Twain, American humorist*

Three men agree to pay two kids for the use of their boat, so they can get to the other side of a river. The boat is small, and can't carry all of them across in one trip, so the men agree to pay the kids one dollar for each crossing, with the proviso that the kids will end up on the same side of the river they started from.

The maximum capacity of the boat is 150 pounds. Each man weighs 150 pounds and each kid weighs 75 pounds. They're all capable of rowing the boat single-handedly across the river.

Clearly, they'll have to make a series of crossings to get all three men across and both kids back to the starting point. Note, however, that the boat can carry one man alone, two kids together (or one kid alone); but it cannot carry more than one man.

Figure out how much it will cost (how many crossings it will take) to get all three men to the other side and both boys back to the starting point, considering the limitation of the boat's carrying capacity. *Don't read the answer below until you try it.*

(Answer: the number of dollars is the number of eggs in a dozen.)

"We are discreet sheep; we wait to see how the drove is going, and then we go with the drove. We have two opinions: one private, which we are afraid to express; and another one – the one we use – which we force ourselves to wear to please Mrs. Grundy, until habit makes us comfortable in it, and the custom of defending it presently makes us love it, adore it, and forget how pitifully we come by it."

~ *Mark Twain, American humorist*

Understanding: a Simple Poem

A long time ago I wrote this short message, as a reflection on the transience of human experience. It's been reprinted many times since.

Understanding

Your values are not my values;

Your thoughts are not my thoughts.

You have come here by a long and winding path,

as have I.

Our paths may cross, but they are not the same path.

You believe as you do, you feel as you do, you react as you do,

Because you have traveled your own path;

And I have traveled mine.

If I can accept you and your values,

Your beliefs and your reactions;

Respond to you as you are – not as I would like you to be;

If I can grant the sovereignty of your values

And you can grant the sovereignty of mine,

Then we have the beginning of understanding.

~ Karl Albrecht, 1975

You can download a printable poster version of this poem at:

http://www.KarlAlbrecht.com/downloads/Albrecht-Understanding.pdf.

We'll Be Ready For 'Em

There are some GORBAs (good ole red-blooded Americans) up in Idaho and a few other places, who are training regularly for the day – and it will come, they're sure – when the UN comes to take over America.

They're the same patriots who diligently report the flyovers of those black helicopters.

And their logic is unassailable.

You just know that, when the UN troops come to take over, the very first place they'll have to land is right up there in Spudknuckle, Idaho, or maybe Flyspeck, South Dakota.

The UN invaders are clued in – they know that Bubba and his Millennium Militia forces will pose the most dangerous threat of all. They'll have to land up there and wipe them out first.

And commander Bubba will be ready for 'em – if his wife lets him out of the house.

The "Popeye" Point

Rock singer Tina Turner endured years of physical and emotional abuse from her husband and co-performer Ike Turner. Like so many people in similar situations, she had been unable to muster up the determination to break out of the soul-destroying situation that was imprisoning her.

Then one day, after a particularly violent episode, something suddenly changed inside her. She became a different Tina Turner. She abruptly made a life-changing decision. She walked out and never came back.

Tina Turner had come to the "Popeye" point.

The metaphor refers to the long-surviving cartoon character Popeye (the sailor man), familiar to most Americans but maybe not to others. He's a good-natured, easy-going guy who tries to get through life as peacefully and cheerfully as possible. In the animated cartoon episodes, his emotional fortitude is always being tested by mean, nasty, abusive people around him, some of whom like to whale on him physically.

At a certain point in each episode, he reaches his tipping point ("That's all I can stands – I can't stands no more!"), after which he blows up. He whips out a can of spinach, downs it in one gulp, flexes his muscles, and then mops the floor with his tormenters.

I refer to that instant of self-assertion, metaphorically, as the Popeye point. I imagine that almost every functioning adult has had one or more big Popeye experiences during his or her life. I've tried to study some of mine, and I've been intrigued by what I've found. I want to learn more about this unique and intriguing psychological event.

More closely defined, the Popeye point is that instant at which a person (you, me, we) decides to break out of an imprisoning life situation and asserts his or her own interests. It could be a bad marriage, an abusive relationship, a lousy job, a wrong business situation, an attachment to smoking, food, or . . . ?

There seem to be three key features of the Popeye experience:

1. There's a period of being "stuck" – unable to muster up the determination to change one's circumstances.

2. The decision to change comes suddenly – a flash of inspiration / determination / clarity, which I believe originates at some preconscious or visceral level, not the level of conscious processing.

3. The decision becomes irreversible; it's a permanent change.

Have you had some big Popeye points in your life? How do you remember them? Can you recall, in a deep, visceral sense, how you felt before the flash, and how you felt afterward?

What, if anything, have your Popeye experiences taught you?

Who Writes Those Headlines?

Smart-asses? Or, dumb-asses?

Something Went Wrong in Jet Crash, Experts Say

Police Begin Campaign to Run Down Jaywalkers

Iraqi Head Seeks Arms

Prostitutes Appeal to Pope

British Left Waffles on Falkland Islands

Plane Too Close to Ground, Crash Probe Told

Miners Refuse to Work After Death

War Dims Hope for Peace

If Strike Isn't Settled Quickly, It May Last a While

Couple Slain; Police Suspect Homicide

Man Struck by Lightning Faces Battery Charge

Typhoon Rips Through Cemetery; Hundreds Dead

Two Sisters Reunited after 18 Years in Checkout Line

Favorite Lame Joke # 9

A young couple had been discussing the option of having a child together. She was keen on the idea, but he wasn't.

After some months, she finally persuaded him to go along with it, and to refrain from using the condom.

On the evening of the first attempt at pregnancy, their union was unusually passionate.

During the heat of passion, she didn't notice that he had slipped on a condom before climbing into bed.

After the festivities, he stepped into the bathroom to dispose of the evidence. She was lying in bed, enjoying the dreamy afterglow of their liaison. She called out to him, "Honey, if we have a boy, what would you like to name him?"

As he dropped the condom into the wastebasket, he muttered under his breath, "Well, if he gets out of this, we'll call him Houdini."

How's the Wedding Business?

Fifty percent of adult Americans are single.

Mental Jelly Beans # 3

Attributed to Comedian Steven Wright:

- ❖ Honk if you love peace and quiet.

- ❖ Sometimes I feel like I'm diagonally parked in a parallel universe.

- ❖ I got a humidifier and a de-humidifier. I put them in the same room and closed the door – let 'em fight it out.

- ❖ I wonder how much deeper the ocean would be without all those sponges?

- ❖ If Barbie is so popular, why do you have to buy her friends?

- ❖ Is it true that cannibals don't eat clowns because they taste funny?

- ❖ Nothing is foolproof to a talented fool.

- ❖ The problem with the gene pool is that there is no lifeguard.

- ❖ Why do they put Braille on the drive-through bank machines?

- ❖ Why don't sheep shrink when it rains?

"Being on the tightrope is living; everything else is waiting."

~ *Karl Wallenda, legendary high-wire performer*

Famous Bad Calls # 3

Are literary critics failed writers? History offers lots of examples of "experts" who ridiculed authors who later became famous. As the oft-quoted Greek philosopher Anonymous reminds us, there are very few statues erected in honor of critics.

Here are a few notoriously bad calls:

"The most ridiculous, insipid play I ever saw in my life."

~ *Samuel Pepys,* British public official, after seeing Shakespeare's "Midsummer Night's Dream," 1662

"Moby-Dick is sad stuff, dull and dreary, or ridiculous. Mr. Melville's Quakers are the wretchedest dolts and drivellers, and his Mad Captain . . . is a monstrous bore."
~ *The Southern Quarterly Review, 1851*

"We fancy that any real child might be more puzzled than enchanted by this stiff, overwrought story."
~ *Review by Children's Books*, of *Alice's Adventures in Wonderland*, 1865

"I'm sorry, Mr. Kipling, but you just don't know how to use the English language."
~ *Editor of the San Francisco Examiner*, rejecting Rudyard Kipling's article, 1889

"A hundred years from now it is very likely that [of all Mark Twain's works] 'The Jumping Frog' alone will be remembered."
~ *Harry Thurston Peck*, editor of *The Bookman*, 1901

"No legs, no jokes, no chance."
~ *Michael Todd*, Broadway producer, after seeing a tryout performance of "Oklahoma!" in 1943. The play ran for 2,248 performances and became one of the best-loved shows of all time.

"There is not much demand for animal stories in the U.S.A."
~ *The Dial Press*, rejecting George Orwell's offer of the American publishing rights to *Animal Farm*, 1944

"Irving Berlin's score is musically not exciting; of the real songs, only one or two are tuneful."
~ *Lewis Kronenberger*, theater critic, reviewing the Broadway opening of "Annie Get Your Gun," 1946. The play ran for 1,147 performances, and gave America at least 7 of its most popular tunes, including "There's No Business Like Show Business," "The Girl That I Marry," and "Doin' What Comes Naturally."

"Who would want to see a play about an unhappy traveling salesman? Too depressing."

~ *Cheryl Crawford*, turning down Elia Kazan's offer to stage Arthur Miller's drama, "Death of a Salesman," 1948

"[George Orwell's] *1984* is a failure."

~ *Laurence Brander*, literary critic, 1954

Steve Jobs: the Lone Genius?

The "Steve Jobs as genius" narrative has a lot going for it – simplicity, drama, mystery, irony, and cult of personality. But, while we're indulging in our post-mortem adoration of this semi-tragic hero, let's ask: what might Apple – and Steve Jobs – have been without the cast of complementary thinkers who contributed through their unique ways of knowing? Much has been said about Jobs' vision and temperament, but little about his pattern of nonlinear thinking.

Steve Jobs needed Steve Wozniak. Jobs' preferred thinking pattern was what I call *Red Sky* – right-brained (intuitive), and abstract (conceptual, philosophical, idealistic). This pattern (one of my four primary *Mindex* thinking styles) is not one we usually associate with high-tech people.

That's why Jobs needed Steve Wozniak, or someone like him, to bring his ideas down to earth and put wheels on them. Wozniak, I believe, was a *Blue Earth* thinker – left-brained (logical, analytical, structured), and concrete (focused on direct experience and tangible outcomes). They made a successful combination, especially during Apple's start-up phase.

Jobs-watchers, biographers, and historians seem to like to characterize him as the tyrannical genius, who did all the thinking, called all the shots, and hounded people to do things his way. That narrative makes good legend literature, but it's oversimplified.

Several other remarkable thinkers contributed crucially to the Apple story, each adding something to the constellation of possibilities swirling around Jobs and Wozniak. Jobs, to his credit, supplied the obsessive motivational energy that animated the enterprise.

Jobs and Woz needed others. As early as 1977, they recognized their lack of business acumen, and turned to a silicon valley engineering executive, Armas Clifford (Mike) Markkula, who had retired at age 32 from Fairchild Semiconductor with a sackful of money. Markkula brought not only the seed capital, but the thinking process that turned the geek-shop into a billion-dollar business.

Markkula provided the *Blue Sky* thinking pattern – logical and abstract – that Jobs and Woz lacked. Blue Sky thinkers tend to be architectural visionaries who frame grand ideas in terms of the sequence and timing of events required to bring them to fruition. Jobs played the dreamer, Woz played the gifted bench-tinkerer, and Markkula served as the planner. Markkula served as chairman from 1985 to 1997. In 1993 he reluctantly joined with CEO John Sculley in ousting Jobs from the firm. Eventually, he also helped force Sculley out.

Another less-known genius who provided a key part of the brain trust was Jef Raskin, a high-altitude sky thinker (Blue Sky and Red Sky patterns working in tandem). Raskin played a seminal role in the invention of the Macintosh computer, and reportedly introduced Jobs to the pioneers of the graphic interface at Xerox's Palo Alto research facility. As early as 1981, Raskin envisioned computers for the millions, and conceived of product incarnations that even foreshadowed today's iPad and other portable devices.

Others completed the picture. During Apple's Camelot phase, other bright thinkers of various patterns made crucial but largely unsung contributions. *Red Earth* whiz-kids (intuitive and concrete) crafted innovative product styles and designs. Many of their ideas set the standard for today's products.

Jobs' abrasive personality might be explained in part by his frustration in trying to make himself understood by others. His associates may not have arranged their mental furniture as he did. Ideas and conclusions that seemed obvious to him may not have fit well with their thinking styles. Like many Red Sky thinkers, Jobs felt like the proverbial stranger in a strange land. When you're bright and your ideas outrun your words, you can become very frustrated when people don't understand you.

None of this diminishes Jobs' contributions. But history has a way of simplifying the big stories. Historians, like journalists, tend to dislike stories with too many heroes. They prefer to raise up one towering figure and summarize the contributions of the rest.

"The world is a tragedy to those who feel,
and a comedy to those who think."
~ *Horace Walpole, British statesman*

☆ ☆ ☆ ☆ ☆

They Didn't Miss Him at Work?

> 10h   The Indian government fired a civil servant who **went on
> sick leave in 1990** and never came back to work. He had
> been under investigation since 1992 for abusing his leave.
> BBC News »

I'll bet he had a big pile of work waiting for him when he came in.

Practical Prose

Some time in the late 1800s, American news reporters gravitated toward the "pyramid" style of organizing the stories they submitted.

Pyramid compositions had a single "big-idea" paragraph at the beginning, briefly summarizing the story. Then followed a series of paragraphs giving further details, delving to ever deeper levels of the story.

The reader could get a quick idea of the gist of the story, and could choose to read further or bail out if he or she had learned enough.

This method had another important advantage, over and above convenience for the reader.

With the rise of the telegraph as the dominant technology platform for moving information around, reporters could file their stories from hundreds of miles away from the big-city newspaper offices.

However, according to traditional accounts of the day, the telegraph service could be unreliable. A common cause of the malfunctions was that Native Americans (Indians, as they were

188

called in those days) took a liking to the copper wires strung along the telegraph poles marching across the landscape.

They would climb the poles, pull down the wires, and use the copper to make all sorts of useful items such as jewelry and personal decorations.

Reporters, knowing that their stories might have to be re-telegraphed and repeated through several links to get to the editorial offices, made sure enough of the story got through on the first try so that the editors would have at least a well-packaged summary to work with.

Ah, them pesky Indians – what to do about them?

"A little sincerity is a dangerous thing,

and a great deal of it can be absolutely fatal."

~ *Oscar Wilde, British novelist, poet*

Factoids # 6

❖ The Eiffel Tower, in Paris, gets taller in hot weather by as much as six inches. No wonder you get more tired climbing it during the summer.

❖ The *scarlet ibis*, a bird native to several Latin American countries, gets its brilliant red coloration from eating lots of tiny crabs that have red shells. Without this food supply, their feathers fade to a nondescript gray.

❖ Scientists estimate that the total population of ants in the world would weigh just about the same as the population of humans. Yes, there are people who spend their time figuring out things like that.

❖ Only about 35 percent of Americans have passports, according to the U.S. State Department. That compares to 60 percent for Canadians and 75 percent for citizens of the United Kingdom. Fifty percent of the trips Americans take in a typical year are to Canada or Mexico, which don't require passports. Clearly, most Americans are not particularly avid world explorers.

- ❖ Only twelve human beings have ever walked on the moon, and all within a three-year period, 1969 through 1972. As of this writing, no one has ever gone back.

- ❖ Lotteries are big business in America. In a typical recent year, state lotteries took in $53.1 billion in ticket sales, and paid out $32.8 billion, a gross profit margin of almost 40 percent. With administrative costs averaging about 5–7 percent, they still keep over one-third of the revenue. Most states use the profits for education and other public services. States have another advantage: they often pay out the prizes over extended periods, in some cases 10 or 20 years. They benefit from interest earned on the funds they hold over that time, and from the long-term effects of inflation.

- ❖ A typical active human being will probably walk a total distance about equal to four times around the Earth, in his or her lifetime.

PBI # 24: A Nickel for Your Thoughts?

It's probably time to phase out the American penny. It long ago outlived its usefulness as a denomination for small amounts of money. Now it's just an historical holdover from a bygone day.

Here's an interesting mental exercise: how many effects or impacts can you think of that might be caused by eliminating the penny? Here are a few to start with:

- o Gasoline stations would probably have to drop the fiction of setting prices to the penny, or even a fraction of a penny.

- o Merchants wouldn't be able to hoodwink their customers into thinking something costs "about nine dollars" by pricing it at $9.99.

- o Accounting systems would probably have far fewer errors, because the last digit of every number would be either a zero or a five. Clerks could add figures in their heads much faster.

- o Cash registers wouldn't need the penny tray. Cashiers would spend less time restocking, counting them, and wrapping them.

190

- o There would probably be fewer back injuries amongst armed guards who transport cash around; pennies add a lot of weight for the small amount of value they represent.

Of course, some people might grieve for the loss of their favorite clichés or slogans: "A nickel for your thoughts" doesn't sound as poetic, although it might seem more respectful. "Nickel-wise and pound-foolish" sounds a bit strange, too. And, somehow, "Nickel" doesn't sound like a very pretty name for a woman.

Still, progress is progress. I'll probably miss it, though.

Change Your Words and You Change Your World

Former actress Robin Givens, interviewed for a *Time* magazine article about partner abuse by celebrity athletes, described her experience of being beaten by heavyweight boxer Mike Tyson. Her choice of words reveals a verbal pattern that's one of the telltale markers for the mindset of powerlessness. In the conceptual realm of *psychosemantics*, it's known as *displacement* – switching from "I" pronouns to "you" pronouns.

Note the alternation between the two patterns in her quotes:

> "People ask why I didn't leave after I was hit the first time . . . But *you* feel such inner turmoil and confusion. *You* want it to be only one time."

> "And for three days after that incident I did the right thing. I said, 'Don't call me. I never want to see you again.' . . . But then *you* start taking his phone calls. Then he asks to see *you* in person, and *you* say yes to that. Then *you* have a big giant man crying like a baby on your lap, and next thing *you* know, *you're consoling him.*"

The pronoun switching, typically unconscious, has the effect of priming the listener's forgiveness, by projecting the inclination for the same self-defeating behavior onto the listener. "You might have done the same thing," the syntax implies; "it wasn't my fault." This is a fairly typical psychosemantic maneuver of *abdication* – surrendering the authority and responsibility to act in one's own self-interest.

Listen to people who have power in and over their lives, and compare the language they use to the language of those who, for whatever reason, may feel disempowered. You're likely to hear two subtly different narratives. One is the narrative of cause and effect. The other, figuratively, is the narrative of "effect and cause."

Getting behind the words for a moment, we can recognize two distinctly different mindsets, or mental states. When someone is at the place of "cause," psychologically speaking, he or she acts from an intention, seeks an outcome, and has a plan, however elementary it might be.

And when one is at the place of "effect," one perceives and conceives of himself or herself as on the receiving end of the intentions and actions of others. Things are done *to* this person, not *by* them.

Let's not over-generalize: Being "at effect" has its value at times. When someone is giving you a massage or some other pleasant sensory experience, "effect" is a great place to be. Being nurtured, comforted, and cared for can be a very satisfying experience.

The strategic choice, moment to moment, is whether to act from the *place of cause* or the *place of effect*. On average, you're more powerful in your life when you act and react from the place of cause. Conversely, you may be a victim in your life to the extent that you refuse to take responsibility for your behavior and its consequences. Language behavior is just as real and revealing as any other kind of behavior. It telegraphs its state of origin.

So can you really change your attitudes about life just by changing the words you use to frame your thoughts? It might sound a bit simplistic, but consider that the structure of your language is the software of your brain – or, at least, one important kind of software.

Which comes first, a thought – or the words that frame it? Many semanticists would claim that they arise simultaneously in the brain. When we habitually say something in a certain way, we're predisposed to think about it in terms of the subtle implications of the words we've chosen. Language evokes thought, and thought evokes language.

You might begin by listening more carefully for the subtle cues of cause and effect – capacity and incapacity – in the conversations around you. "My girlfriend treats me like dirt"; "My parents never let me do what I want to"; "Yes, he has a bad temper, but I can't leave him right now; he needs me"; "I was trying to lose weight, but I fell off the wagon"; "I can't afford that right now."

The language of powerlessness seems to pervade much of the popular culture and its discourse, even its music. And not just today: Remember, one of Frank Sinatra's best-known songs was "You're Nobody 'til Somebody Loves You."

Too many political activists today preach a victim narrative to their target audiences. "Society," they tell their listeners, is somehow holding them back, keeping them down, preventing them from participating in the good life. But maybe it's really the activists, and their disempowering narrative, holding them back.

There's a lot more to the psychology of cause and effect, but a good starting point for most of us would be to clean up our language. The famous motivational psychologist Norman Vincent Peale often said, "Change your thoughts, and you change your world." Maybe it's time to update that advice:

Change your words, and you change your world.

Let Them Ride Bikes?

Corporate executives in the wealthy countries are beginning to worry about the growing competition for oil-based energy from the developing countries. As people in China, India, and Brazil start to get ahead of their conditions, they inevitably seem to want cars. And cheaply made cars for the masses will consume more gasoline as well as produce lots more pollution.

What to do? Well, they might be able to delay the rising competition for oil for a decade or more, by a very simple method. *They could just give free bicycles to the people of those countries*, which would provide them with cheap transportation for the short run. At a base manufacturing cost of about $30 per bicycle, one billion bikes would cost about $30 billion, which is about one month's cost of oil consumption in the United States. They could also locate the bike factories in the target countries, thus creating jobs.

Might be a good trade-off for corporations in the wealthy economies.

Or, maybe not . . .

"Some people are more certain about everything than I am about anything."

~ *Robert Rubin*

"History doesn't repeat itself,

but it does rhyme."

~ *Mark Twain*

PBI # 25: How Green is Your Greeting?

The average useful life of a typical greeting card seems like about seven seconds. If it gets passed around at the birthday or retirement party, it might live to the ripe old age of two minutes. Then it's history – headed for the dustbin.

It's hard to think of any other type of product that does so little, in such a short time, at such a high ecological cost.

Online greeting cards are now competing with printed cards, partly because of the conservation considerations, and also mostly because they're an easy and obvious way of using information technology.

Shall we abolish the printed greeting card altogether, save trees, and protect the birds nesting in them? Or could we salvage it somehow? Should we try? At this point, there's almost no ecological justification for a greeting card that gets thrown away after a few seconds. I've stopped buying them altogether.

However, we might be able to change the eco-logic in favor of the cardboard version, by extending its useful life and having it serve other purposes. Could we, for example:

➤ Make it reusable?

➤ Make it edible?

➤ Make it do double duty as an electronic gift card?

➤ Make it plantable – glue some seeds to the back, make it degradable in water, and have it serve as a fertilizer?

What other rescue possibilities can you think of?

✪ ✪ ✪ ✪ ✪

"We're in science fiction now, man. Whoever controls the images – the media – controls the culture."

~ *Allen Ginsberg, beat poet*

✪ ✪ ✪ ✪ ✪

Favorite Lame Joke # 10

A young couple had made plans to go to a costume party hosted by the leaders of the social club they'd been thinking of joining.

Having recently moved into town, they knew very few of the people who would be there, and they felt this would be a good opportunity to begin to mingle with the social set.

An hour before departure time, he had on his gorilla suit and was ready to go.

"I'm not feeling very well, honey," she said. "I think I'll just stay home and get to bed early, but please go and make an appearance on my behalf. Have a good time."

So, off he went.

About two hours later, she was feeling considerably better, and decided she'd go to the party after all.

She put on her costume, that of a Victorian-age society woman with a voluminous ball gown, high wig, and full face mask.

As she was driving to the party, it occurred to her that she hadn't told him what costume she planned to wear.

"I think I'll surprise him," she thought. "Even better, I'll check him out to see if he can be tempted to get cozy with a strange woman who comes on to him."

Entering the party, she spotted the gorilla costume immediately, and began to make her way toward him. She grabbed his hand and pulled him out onto the dance floor.

As they danced, she began to give him all the usual signals of availability. They danced more closely, rubbing together, and getting ever more overheated.

Then she led him out onto the terrace, which was mostly abandoned. One thing led to another and they were soon hiding in the shrubbery, engaged in some serious physical interaction.

After things cooled down, she parted from him as quickly as possible, leaving him to wonder what had brought him such good fortune.

She drove home, with a mischievous plan in mind. She hid the costume, showered, and changed into her night clothes.

When he came in, she invited him to have coffee and a late snack in the kitchen.

"So," she asked, rather nonchalantly, "Did you enjoy the party?"

"Oh, it was OK," he replied, casually.

"Meet anyone interesting?" she inquired.

"Well no – actually, it wasn't much fun without you there, so I just sat in the kitchen with some other guys and we played cards all evening."

"Oh?" she inquired, wondering how best to trap him into a confession. But before she could set the bait, he had a bit more to add.

". . . but the guy I loaned the gorilla suit to – boy, he had a great time!"

"A beautiful theory, murdered by a gang of brutal facts."

~ *Thomas Huxley, English scientist and philosopher*

Is it Time to Phase Out the Business Suit?

Sociologists refer to distinctive items of clothing, or styles of dress, as *class marks* – signals that tell others how the individual wants to be perceived, and with which socio-ethnic group he or she wants to affiliate.

Baseball caps, rugby shirts, hip-hop outfits, spike heels, military uniforms, and business suits are all class marks. So are certain hairstyles, cosmetics, pierced body parts, and tattoos.

The business suit seems to convey the idea that the wearer is socially and economically above the common people – someone who doesn't have to get his or hands dirty.

Ironically, one who is ultra-rich and ultra-famous can acquire the right to leave the business suit behind and adopt the class marks of the "lower classes." Facebook CEO Mark Zuckerberg, for example, wears the street-geek uniform of a black T-shirt, or a hoodie. Famous author Stephen King wears just about any damned thing he likes. Many successful stand-up comics wear T-shirts and jeans.

Of course, being exempt from conventional class-marks can sometime force different class marks on people. Would people think something was strange if Robin Williams had performed his comedy routines wearing a tuxedo? Would Zuckerberg lose his geek identity if he changed his outfit?

Businesses are gradually moving toward "casual dress" days, and even casual dress appearance codes. Does this change tend to minimize or blur the differences in rank and status, or will it give rise to other ways of expressing them?

Just wondering . . .

"It takes a very unusual mind to make an analysis of the obvious."

~ *Alfred North Whitehead, English mathematician & philosopher*

PBI # 26: So, You Might Get Poisoned? Big Deal

Have Americans become a nation of wimps and milquetoasts? Are we so over-protected that we've become soft and complacent?

Every time some company confesses that they've been selling contaminated food products, for example – burgers, fruits, vegetables, meat, eggs, baby formula – the government goes into recall mode and consumers go into an hysterical state of avoidance. Millions and millions of packages of perfectly good food are recalled and destroyed, along with the bad stuff.

But think about it: out of a billion eggs, only a few of them are suspected – we never know how many – to be contaminated with salmonella bacteria. That can kill people, but realistically, only a very few would actually get sick or die. The vast majority of the other people, who would eat the eggs that don't have the bacteria, would never be affected. This is bad economics. Starving people in poor countries would probably rather take the gamble.

As usual, I've got a better plan. Suppose that, every time a company gets caught with contaminated food, they have to put up a big hunk of cash to pay the victims. Considering the huge costs and disruption of a recall, even a large fund would still probably be much cheaper than the recall.

The government would announce and publicize the problem of the contaminated food, and people could decide for themselves whether to buy and eat the product. If someone got sick, they – or their heirs – would file a claim and get a big payment, like a pay-out on an insurance policy. Sort of like a lottery.

If you're a risk-taker, you might gamble on getting rich – or making your family rich, if you don't survive. If you're more cautious, you can just decide not to eat the product that's in trouble at the moment.

There might be some interesting side effects of this solution. I suppose the gene pool for risk-takers might get smaller. And I suppose it's possible that people with suicidal tendencies might be attracted to the program.

But, hey – those are details. Every great idea has a few little bugs.

Vicious Animals

The meanest animal on the planet is an unmated human male between the ages of 15 and 25.

Why We Believe What We Believe

We all have mental *biases* – a lot more of them than we prefer to admit.

What's a bias?

It's an "ABCDE" – an *Assumption, Belief, Conclusion, Decision, or Emotion* that distorts our perceptions and narrows our options for responding to experience.

Most people raised in the Anglo–Western cultures like to think of themselves as "objective" – unbiased, logical, and sensible. Most of us learn from early childhood to think of ourselves as seeking the "right" answers at the many decision points we encounter. Moment by moment, day by day, we want to believe that we analyze things skillfully and base our opinions and our behavior on the correct conclusions.

Reality – to say nothing of research – contradicts that belief routinely.

Wikipedia.com lists over 75 named biases that psychologists find interesting enough to study.

One of the most pervasive of these is the simple *confirmation bias* (a.k.a. *selective perception bias*) – the tendency to pay closer attention to evidence and arguments that support one's firmly held conclusions, and to avoid or discount contradictory evidence. This one phenomenon could partially explain the tendency of large numbers of people to hold fast to their attachments to one political party or another. Once we decide, we don't like to re-decide.

Some cognitive researchers suggest that the brain has to consume extra energy in the process of changing or rearranging its beliefs, and that neurological laziness – the tendency to conserve glucose and oxygen – predisposes the brain to hold on to the configurations it already has.

The pervasive media culture, and lately the social media component, provide endless opportunities for people to take on beliefs, impressions, and biases that are completely erroneous. Partisan political journalism, in particular, routinely trades in distortions, tortured facts, selective evidence, and downright lies. Once a fraudulent "factoid" gets launched, passing on from one diatribe to another, it can acquire the status of unquestioned truth. We might think of the *big-lie* bias, or the *repetition bias* as a powerful one, because no one can reasonably expect to verify the accuracy or plausibility of every such proposition he or she encounters. Media manipulators capitalize on that mechanism every day.

"Net-crud," the contrived photographs and stories circulating on the Internet, have been deliberately manufactured or doctored so as to mislead readers into thinking of them as evidence of remarkable discoveries or events. Claims attributed to "ex-CIA

199

agents," "retired FBI agents," or "ex-NASA engineers" attempt to borrow legitimacy for the fabricated claims. So many people have grown up with a moral injunction against lying that they automatically assume that a remarkable story or claim must be true. It's hard for them to consider that some people willingly lie. Researchers identify this affliction, simply, as *gullibility bias.*

Cognitive researchers also identify a *backfire bias*, the tendency of some people – particularly those with cult-like beliefs – to actually strengthen their beliefs or convictions in the face of overwhelming disconfirmation. "I don't care what anybody says, UFOs (or ghosts, or bigfoot, or angels, etc.) are real."

The *"Lake Wobegon" bias* – "All the children are above average" – leads many parents to overestimate the talents of their kids. "She could do a lot better in school if she'd just work harder."

There's a *knew-it-all-the-time bias*, which is the tendency to look back on events or situations and believe that one understood them better than was actually the case. "I knew this was bound to happen, because . . ."

Affinity bias is the tendency to believe or agree with the ideas of people you like or admire, and to discount or disagree with those you dislike.

There's also the *reactance bias*, which is the tendency to do the opposite of what someone advises you or wants you to do. This usually reflects an aversion to loss of autonomy, i.e. concern about being pushed around, controlled, or coerced.

How about *bias bias*? That's the tendency to believe that other people are more biased than you are. Do you find yourself attributing the beliefs or behaviors of others to biases you assign to them? Can you identify the biases of your own that might arise in similar situations?

There are lots more biases where those come from. If you find the notion of biases and biased behavior intriguing or relevant to your life, you can read up on the popular literature of rational and irrational behavior.

And, of course, you can start by tuning up your perceptual radar to detect possible biases that show up in the behavior of others. And particularly, you might begin to trace out more of your own biases by observing more closely the things you say and do every day.

Look up: http://en.wikipedia.org/wiki/List_of_cognitive_biases

✪ ✪ ✪ ✪ ✪

"There is no right way to do the wrong thing."

~ *Thomas Huxley, British scientist & philosopher*

✪ ✪ ✪ ✪ ✪

Driving Defensively

Don't you find it annoying, and even stressful, when you're driving your car and some eager beaver crowds you from behind? He stays within a car-length or two, presumably trying to pressure you to go faster.

Well, I'm working on the solution to that problem. It's an after-market product you'll be able to buy and have installed on your car. It dispenses a puff of evil-smelling gas, consisting mostly of hydrogen sulfide, for that great "rotting vegetation / rotten eggs" smell.

When he roars up behind you, and hangs there at a dangerously close distance, you just push the button on your dashboard and the car – well – "farts."

My design team considered adding methane gas to the mixture, which is what's contained in human intestinal gas – make it more realistic, you know.

However, methane is flammable, and it might get drawn up into his engine compartment, ignite, and maybe blow the hood off his car.

Maybe a bit too extreme.

For full effect, the product might include a speaker with various options for flatulent sounds, like that low-pitched tuba blast; or the sound of a big truck horn; or maybe the horn sound of a big ship.

Somebody's gotta come up with these solutions, right?

✪ ✪ ✪ ✪ ✪

"I often quote myself; it adds spice to my conversation."

~ *George Bernard Shaw*

✪ ✪ ✪ ✪ ✪

✪ ✪ ✪ ✪ ✪

You are here.

✪ ✪ ✪ ✪ ✪

Nitwitticisms # 5

"The streets are safe in Philadelphia. It's only *the people* who make them unsafe."

~ *Frank Rizzo*, ex-police chief and mayor of Philadelphia

"And here's Moses Kiptanui, a 19-year-old Kenyan, who turned 20 a few weeks ago."

~ *Sportscaster David Coleman*

"Sundance [Film Festival] is weird. The movies are weird. You actually have to think about them when you watch them."

~ *Pop singer Britney Spears*

"I have made good judgments in the past. I have made good judgments in the future."

~ *U.S. Vice President Dan Quayle*

"For NASA, space is still a high priority."

~ *U.S. President George W. Bush*

Interviewer from *Rolling Stone magazine*: "What was the best thing you read all year?"

Answer: "You mean, like, a book?"

~ *Singer Justin Timberlake*

"Instructions: Open Packet, Eat Nuts."

~ *Printed on a packet of nuts, served on American Airlines flight*

What Will They Think of Next?

> 16h   Electric roller skates, a tea kettle with Wi-Fi and a 3-D
> printer for cookies are among the gadgets unveiled at the
> **International Consumer Electronics Show** in Las Vegas.
> Wired ⌇

In my early days as an engineer, we had a favorite expression: "The sheer technical brilliance of it obscures its utter uselessness."

"Problems are the price of progress. Don't bring me anything but trouble. Good news weakens me."

~ *Charles F. Kettering* (American engineer, inventor of the electric starter)

Freeing Yourself From Toxic Loops

The simple decision to *stop arguing* with people can set you free.

Stan Laurel and Oliver Hardy, the famous comedy duo, made a priceless film in 1927, portraying themselves as entrepreneurs trying to sell Christmas trees door-to-door in Los Angeles.

At their first stop, they got a rude rejection from a curmudgeonly resident. Offended by his attitude, they repeatedly rang his doorbell and re-solicited his business. Finally, in frustration, he grabbed the tree they were offering and threw it into the street.

Outraged, they tore off his porch light. Reciprocally outraged, he rushed out to the street and ripped off the headlight from their truck.

Things quickly escalated. At each cycle, they did something more damaging to his house, to which he responded by perpetrating further violence on their truck. Soon they had pretty well thrashed his house, and he had turned their truck into a pile of wreckage.

The police got involved, and – well, you'd have to see it to appreciate it.

This little fifteen-minute drama recapitulates one of the oldest, most painful dynamics of the human experience: the escalating tit-for-tat conflict in which each of the protagonists believes him- or herself to be the aggrieved party. I call it the *toxic loop*. After showing the Laurel and Hardy film in a workshop on social intelligence, I like to ask two questions: 1) Who started it? and 2) Who won?

Toxic loops are remarkably common in everyday human interaction. The dissatisfied customer says something sarcastic, to which the service employee reacts in kind. A simple conversation between a husband and wife hits a snag and turns into a bitter argument – often over nothing of consequence. An aggressively expressed political opinion triggers a heated debate, with the exchange of ever increasing personal insults. A supervisor points out some shortfall in job performance, the employee responds aggressively, and they fall into a cycle of trading accusations.

Many years ago I made an important personal decision: *to stop arguing with people*. I consider it one of the most valuable decisions I've ever made. It has freed me from stress, negative feelings, and the compulsive need to "be right." I didn't give up on influencing other people, or inviting them to change their minds – I just acknowledged the futility of trying to bully them into agreeing with me.

We can't hope to avoid all conflicts in life – too many circumstances arise in which the purposes of the parties don't match up. But I've often wondered how many of the smaller, everyday negative loops we might prevent or resolve.

We have at least two options for freeing ourselves from toxic loops, and preserving our peace of mind: 1) see them coming, and refuse to be baited into participating; and 2) become aware that we've fallen into them, and simply stop participating. Both require a certain degree of *mindfulness*, a concept that's becoming ever more appealing to enlightened people these days.

The first option might be easier than it seems, once we've turned on our "loop detector." By staying alert for the provocative statement, the sarcastic comment, the accusation – implied or overt – the intolerant or bigoted diatribe, we can make choices about how we will reply. To quote the revered Dalai Lama:

"Sometimes silence is the best answer."

Breaking out of toxic loops once we've fallen into them requires the ability to *self-observe* while engaged with a situation. Our inner voice, which some new-age philosophers refer to as the "observing self," can tell us when we're looping with someone, and remind us that it's going nowhere. Even if the other party or parties don't perceive their imprisonment in the loop, we ourselves always have the choice of individually opting out.

You might say, for example, "Well, I've said everything I have to say," and just fall silent. Or, "I would like to be excused from this conversation." Or, "Could we change the topic? I'm not finding this conversation very fruitful." You might conjure up much more imaginative replies than the examples I've offered.

I suppose our ideas and attitudes about toxic loops reflect our psychic needs related to conflict, doing battle, and winning or losing. I believe that once we let go of the need to be right, we can recall and redirect the psychic energy we've been allowing others to pull from us. We have more options, more possibilities, and more ways to stay centered and use our energy for our own best purposes.

The Chinese philosopher Lao Tzu, credited with writing *The Way of Life*, reportedly said,

"The greatest victor wins without the battle."

PBI # 27: A Cheaper Way to Fight Terrorism?

According to published estimates, the U.S. government spent over a trillion dollars fighting insurgents in Iraq and Afghanistan. The result: probably about 100,000 of them killed – outside estimate. That works out to about *ten million dollars per insurgent.*

To that, also, has to be added the non-monetary cost of 0.1 American soldiers killed per insurgent – nearly 10,000 total, not counting those wounded, maimed, or permanently disabled. Some experts claim that several hundred thousand innocent citizens – including women, children, and the elderly – also lost their lives, and several million more turned into refugees. (But, for the sake of logical analysis, let's just leave out the messy "collateral damage" element.)

What's wrong with this picture?

A cash stipend of just ten thousand dollars, paid to every insurgent, would represent one-thousandth of the cost, with no loss of life, and would amount to a sizable fortune to almost every one of them. That might change their economy so radically that terrorism might lose much of its fuel – the anger of poor people.

Now, I can hear the objections and the push-backs already. "You're rewarding the wrong people." "They'll probably just keep attacking us anyway, with our money." "Everybody in the disturbed country will be applying for the money." "How do we know where the money goes?"

I'm ready for you. It wouldn't be that simple. The payout would come in the form of dollar denominated coupons, redeemable to buy American-made products from American businesses, over the Internet. Each person would have to sign on to Facebook and promise never to commit any act of violence. In addition, they would receive the payout in monthly installments – credits to their PayPal accounts – over a period of ten years.

The online community would police the system. Anyone who received a certain number of "demerits" from other members, based on observed antisocial behavior, would lose his or her credit and get reported to the anti-terrorist authorities. Verified good deeds might earn extra credits.

Of course, American arms manufacturers would probably not be keen on the idea. Maybe they'd have to start buying up consumer-products companies to recapture the revenue. Sort of a "swords into plowshares" kind of thing?

Okay – okay, it's got a few bugs that would have to be worked out. Or, maybe we prefer to keep paying $10,000,000 plus 0.1 American life per insurgent, to keep fighting the mythical "war on terrorism?"

The Party Went Somewhere Else

A key lesson of business is that your most dangerous competitor probably doesn't look like you. It might be somebody or some alternative option that offers your customers something they like better than what you're offering.

Online advertising is a good example.

During the period from 2000 to 2013, advertising revenue for newspapers in the U.S. dropped from about $60 billion to $40 billion. Where did it go?

Well, Google's ad revenue during the same period climbed by $57 billion.

Like a giant vacuum cleaner, the Internet has drawn viewers – and consequently the advertisers who want to get at them – from TV, newspapers, radio, and other traditional media.

"I am afraid to listen, because if I listen, I might understand – and be changed by that understanding."

~ *Carl Rogers, American psychologist*

Should Robots Pay Taxes?

All of the wealthy countries now face the same problem, as yet unsolved: the "demographic see-saw."

As people live longer, there's a growing pile-up in the age range at which they typically retire or can no longer work.

At the same time, birth rates are falling, so there won't be enough young, full-time workers to pay the taxes needed to support the older ones in their later years.

A third change is that technology is steadily eliminating the low-skill – and low-paying – jobs at the bottom of the scale. More and more businesses are robotizing their operations, cutting the number of jobs and thereby cutting incomes.

However, for every job you eliminate, you eliminate a tax contribution. The robots, whether they're physical machines in factories, or software algorithms in computers, don't draw paychecks and don't pay taxes.

So, we may end up with a very labor-efficient economy that can't employ all of the young workers, and doesn't generate enough tax revenue to support the older people at the other end of the see-saw.

Seems like we have two main options: 1) raise the taxes on the ones who work; and 2) levy a tax on robots.

How to tax the robots? Hey – I just do the big thinking; somebody else will have to figure out the details.

Making Workers Love their Work

Sign in a small factory in the West of England:

> **BEATINGS WILL**
>
> **CONTINUE UNTIL**
>
> **MORALE IMPROVES.**

Is the Stock Market a Game for Suckers?

A professor of finance at a major university ran a statistical study to find out how well the typical amateur investor made out in the stock market. He discovered that people who put their money into mutual funds got lower returns, on average, than they would have using the proverbial "dartboard" method. The dartboard approach would be to just tape a list of the companies traded on the stock exchange to a wall, throw a few darts at it, and buy whatever stocks you hit.

How could this be so?

After all, mutual funds are run by full-time investment experts. They pool our money, choose stocks carefully, and manage a portfolio of investments that – supposedly – reduces the individual risk for all of us. Theoretically, we as individuals couldn't possibly invest our little cash-stash better than the pros. Or, could we?

This question was actually answered over 40 years ago by a man named John Bogle, a financial expert who concluded that Wall Street is selling us snake oil. However, the well funded propaganda machine – all the TV shows, magazines, newsletters, blogs, motivational speakers, and word-of-mouth tip-passing – has succeeded in selling most of us on the idea that it's possible to "beat the market."

Bogle saw plainly what brokers and financial advisers don't want the rest of us to notice, namely that mutual funds, on average, *underperform* the dartboard. Another way to say it is that the long-term growth in the popular stock market indexes, such as the *Dow-Jones Industrial Average* and the *Standard & Poor 500* stock average, actually outpaces the long-term growth of all mutual funds.

Why don't mutual funds do better? Even if the people who run them can't make investment calls any better than the dartboard, shouldn't they grow at least as fast as the market indexes?

Two reasons. First, they're constantly taking in new funds, as an army of brokers and investment advisers work diligently every day to sell shares in their funds – collecting a percentage commission on every sale. Who pays the commission? The "investor" – the unwitting sucker who's been conditioned to believe he'll make a good return on his money. These sales commissions – deducted *immediately* from the amount of money you invest – can run from 1 to 5 percent, depending on the size of your stake.

Because mutual fund buyers typically don't hold their shares longer than a few years – about five years on average – those sales commissions chop down their total rate of return by the time they sell.

Second, the people who run the mutual funds deduct yearly "management fees" – typically 1 to 2 percent of the total assets of the fund – for the services they provide.

Add up the sales commissions and the management fees, and consider that you're likely to cash in your shares in about five years or less, and it's obvious that the stocks in the fund's portfolio would have to outperform the dartboard by several percentage points, just to keep up with the indexes.

But it gets worse. The fund's managers feel constant pressure to put the incoming flow of new investor money to work. They can't just hold it as cash, without earning anything. That means they have to keep buying stocks, even when they don't see any good buys.

The last nail in the coffin: irrational investor behavior. The professor running the financial study found that many people switched their mutual fund choices, often on a yearly basis. A typical investor would consult the mutual fund listings, and if his or her fund had performed way below the others, they'd sell their shares and buy the top-performing fund.

This seemingly logical procedure whittled away their assets in two ways. First, it ran up the meter on sales fees, which got deducted directly from their funds – once when they sold, and again when they re-bought. And secondly, because fund performance tends to "porpoise" above and below the average trend line, they were selling on weakness and buying on strength – exactly the opposite of all the advice in the investing books. So, the typical investor does even worse than the mutual funds he or she has been buying and selling.

John Bogle's simple answer to this dilemma: the *index fund*. Run mostly by computers, the fund simply buys and holds stocks in the list of companies that make up a particular index – the Dow-Jones 30 companies, the S&P 500 companies, or others. The fund will never out-perform the dartboard, but it will never under-perform it either. By definition, the rate of return will be exactly the same as the rate of growth in the index it's investing in – minus a very small operating expense.

Ambitious investors might feel impatient with such a reliable but unglamorous approach. If you're one of them, just consider that – statistically, again – opportunistic investors, those who jump in and out of individual stocks, average *significantly lower* than the dartboard, and when they get cleaned, they can really take a bath.

The simple answer is: no, you as an individual can't expect to beat the market. You're just as likely to get clobbered as to strike it rich.

The most reliable stock market strategy is also the cheapest one: the simple index fund, purchased directly.

210

✪ ✪ ✪ ✪ ✪

"You're only given a little spark of madness. You mustn't lose it."

~ *Robin Williams (American comedian)*

✪ ✪ ✪ ✪ ✪

I am a bomb technician. If you see me running, try to keep up.

✪ ✪ ✪ ✪ ✪

PBI # 28: News at Your Fingertips?

The newspaper, as it's commonly sold in the U.S. and most developed countries, is just about the only product we have that's printed on giant sheets of paper. If the newspaper didn't exist in its current form, would we be inclined to invent it?

Every day, hundreds of millions of sheets of newsprint get manufactured, printed, assembled, and delivered – almost all of which get quickly destroyed.

Meanwhile, technology experts are forecasting the extinction, or near extinction, of the newspaper as an information delivery system. And, rightly so, it seems. The local "rag" in my hometown costs two bucks per copy in a newspaper dispenser, and more when the dispenser malfunctions. The only part of it I enjoy reading is the cartoon section – and they're becoming so lame that I skip most of them.

Most of the traditional content in the typical daily newspaper has become obsolete: job opportunities (think monster.com); apartments for rent (think craigslist.com); stock prices (think lots

211

of online sources); recipes for zucchini bread (think lots of cooking websites).

What will kill off the newspaper is not that electronic sources, i.e. screens, are the preferred way to read – they're not. The key factor is that the content is static, pre-determined, and one-size-fits-all.

Prediction: newspapers might be reinvented, to become incarnated as print-on-demand information dispensers, that give each individual the particular package of content he or she requests. Customers could insert smart cards or smart fobs into a slot, and a remote computer would tell the terminal's high-speed printer what information to assemble, how to format it, and how to print and bind it. Never mind putting the coins into a slot – the system would automatically charge the user's account.

And, goodbye to the giant double-folded sheets of paper as the output medium. The commercial world – in the U.S. at least – has standardized on the 8–1/2" x 11" sheet of paper for many years; it works just fine. Color? Sure. Variable resolution? Sure. Tear-out discount coupons? Yup. A font size big enough that you don't have to put on your reading glasses? Easy.

Newspaper dispensers will probably go the way of pay telephones. Any commercial location that receives digital information as part of its function will be a candidate for news dispensing: ATM's; banks; supermarkets; restaurants; stores; maybe even gas stations.

Now, if they can just come up with some better cartoons . . .

Favorite Lame Joke # 11

Adolph Hitler was reportedly rather superstitious, and occasionally consulted astrologers and various mediums (media?) for advice about his future and that of the Third Reich.

In one such episode, he sent his aides out to find the best psychic in all of the German-occupied territories.

They came back with an ancient, gnarled, surly old Jewish man.

"What's this?" Hitler demanded. "Why do you bring me a Jew, for God's sake?"

His chief aide said, "Sorry, Mein Fuehrer, but you told us you wanted the best. Everyone agrees that he's it. He just happens to be a Jew."

"All right," Hitler sighed in frustration.

"Old man," he demanded, "I want you to tell me my future – give me the truth, and don't hold anything back."

The old man said, "Let me see your palm."

Hitler extended his hand, and the old man leaned forward, studying the lines on his hand intently.

"Hoo-hah!" he exclaimed. "I see you're destined to die on a Jewish Holiday."

"Oh, no!" Hitler moaned. "Which holiday will it be?"

The old man gazed at him with a look of defiance and contempt.

"I don't know yet – but any day you die is going to be a Jewish holiday."

Don't Say "Over and Out"

Popular literature, films, and comedy skits sometimes portray military people talking on their radios as saying things like "Over and Out." But people with actual military training don't say that. It would be like saying, "It's your turn to talk now, but I'm not going to listen."

Three of the most common one-word signals for military radio conversations are "Roger," "Over," and "Out."

"Roger" means, "I received your last transmission, I understood it, and I acknowledge that I heard it."

"Over" means, "It's your turn to talk now. I've finished saying what I have to say, and now I'm expecting to hear what you're going to say."

"Out" means, "I'm switching off my radio; that's the end of this conversation for me."

You can say, "Over" – or you can say "Out," but not both in the same transmission. Got it?

Just thought I'd pass on that useful little tip, in case you might find yourself in a combat zone somewhere – or maybe in a movie – and have to talk to somebody over the radio.

"No ray of sunshine is ever lost, but the green which it awakens into existence needs time to grow; and it is not always granted to the sower to see the harvest. All work that is worth anything is done in faith."

~ *Albert Schweitzer, German physician & missionary*

Don't grow up – It's a trap

The First Hundred Years are the Hardest

How do some businesses last a century or more? How can a small enterprise outlast its founders, the next generation, and the next?

A study by Royal Dutch Shell's Arie de Geus, one of the leading thinkers in business strategy, looked at firms that had stayed in business for more than 100 years. He wanted to know whether they had any fundamental secrets to longevity, and what Shell's management would have to do to keep the company going for another century.

He found that the average lifespan of a "Fortune 500" company ran less than 40 years. The average life of all incorporated businesses was about 15 years. Not very encouraging.

After looking at the few big-name firms that had lived past the century mark – Shell, General Electric, Procter & Gamble, Sears, Wall Street firms, and others, he discovered that the several hundred smaller ones had fairly simple formulas: they stuck to what they could do well, and they didn't screw up.

The list had quite a few breweries and wineries, plus specialty manufacturers and miscellaneous others.

An interesting case was McIlhenny & Company, the outfit that makes Tabasco Sauce. Founded in 1868 on Avery Island, Louisiana, their product is nothing more than vinegar mixed with ground peppers and salt; yet they've survived and thrived for all those years.

The oldest firm I could identify in my own research is a Japanese firm, Kongo Gumi, founded *in the year 540* and continuously in business since then. Its business: building and refurbishing Buddhist temples. Imagine having the job of CEO of that company, and waking up every day with the responsibility of fourteen centuries resting on your shoulders. I think that would focus one's awareness wonderfully.

Look up: *The Living Company* by Arie de Geus

"Who can say which will be more important in the end:
landing on the moon, or understanding the human mind?"
~ *Tenzin Gyatso (14th Dalai Lama)*

Factoids # 7

❖ The world population of chickens outnumbers the population of humans. The significance of this fact is not clear.

❖ Most people seem to think of a lightning strike as a rare event. In fact, lightning bolts strike the earth about 5–10 million times a day. A person getting hit by lightning is, however, a rather rare event. Roy Sullivan, a park ranger in the U.S. Shenandoah National Park in Virginia, got hit by lightning on seven different occasions between 1942 and 1977, according to the Guinness World Records book. He died at age 71, from a self-inflicted gunshot wound, over a failed romantic relationship. (Seems like there's a good wisecrack related to this item, but none comes to mind at the moment.)

❖ Your brain consumes about the same amount of energy as a 25-watt bulb. That's a very efficient computer. Your whole body uses about 100 watts, so even though your brain accounts for 2 percent of your body structure, it uses one-fourth of the energy.

❖ The diameter of the moon is about equal to the distance between Los Angeles and New York. Keep that in mind; you might need that little statistic one day.

❖ A supertanker traveling at a typical cruise speed of 16 knots takes about 20 minutes to stop, using conventional braking methods. During that time, it will travel about two to three miles. Using those figures for the *Titanic*, we can see that the crew would have to have spotted the iceberg almost three miles away, in order to avoid hitting it. The iceberg gashed the ship's side as the captain tried desperately to steer around it.

❖ Dolphins reportedly sleep with one eye open. Scientists explain that their brains are divided into two nearly separate "computers," each one receiving input from one eye. Apparently they can put one brain to sleep, while the other controls basic functions such as breathing and watching for predators. I wish I could do that . . .

Is a Diamond Really Forever?

Carol Channing sang the catchy tune, "Diamonds Are a Girl's Best Friend" in 1949, in the original Broadway production of "Gentlemen Prefer Blondes." And Marilyn Monroe made the song eternal in the 1953 film version of the play.

The song immediately became a magic wand for the marketing of diamond jewelry, and it dovetailed perfectly with the durable advertising slogan "A Diamond is Forever."

But the marriage of the song and the slogan was not one made in Heaven. The promotion of diamonds as scarce, precious, fashionable, and essential to a happy human marriage is one of the most remarkable stories in the history the advertising and PR

216

business. And the mastermind behind it was a young woman – who, incidentally, never got married.

Here's the back story.

By the early 1900s, one company – De Beers, in South Africa – had gained control of almost 90 percent of the world's diamond mines. Its founder, Cecil Rhodes, is little known to most Americans, but he ranks on a par with Rockefeller, Carnegie, and the Morgans for sheer monopolistic genius. (He's better known elsewhere as the British-born colonialist who created the concept of *apartheid*, and founded the white-controlled state known as Rhodesia, now renamed Zimbabwe.)

In classic Rockefeller style, Rhodes managed to buy, merge with, or exterminate all of his major competitors, and he forced smaller diamond producers to sell all of their production to his company.

But he had a big problem: he was buying more diamonds than he could sell. The world had changed from a period when diamonds symbolized great wealth and power – even royalty – to a time when they were pouring out of newly discovered mines in India and Africa. Diamond cutters, jewelers, and retailers threatened to make diamonds as abundant as costume jewelry.

Rhodes decided to keep control of the sources of rough diamonds – swooping in to make deals every time a major diamond find opened up in Russia, Australia, and other hot spots – but to choke off the flow to the market place. After he died, the wealthy Oppenheimer family bought the firm and continued the same policy.

By the late 1930s, rough diamond stockpiles were rising and retail sales were falling, partly due to the great Depression, and also due to the thrifty attitudes of young women, who valued the modern conveniences of life – sewing machines, washing machines, electric stoves, and radios – more than jewelry.

Jewelers in most major urban areas relied on "keystone" pricing, which generally meant that they set the retail price of a gem at twice its wholesale cost. De Beers management realized that, if they released their stockpile of diamonds to the market, or even a major part of it, the retail market would crash. They had to continue to restrict the supply, and find ways to increase demand.

This period saw the infancy of the public relations profession, led by the legendary Edward Bernays (a nephew of Sigmund Freud), who turned his World War I propaganda training into a wildly successful career promoting the interests of large corporations (but that's another story for another time).

De Beers contacted the N.W. Ayer advertising agency in New York, asking them to consider whether "the use of propaganda in various forms" might increase the sale of diamonds in the United States. Because De Beers controlled most of the world's supply of rough diamonds, U.S. antitrust laws prohibited the company from doing business there. The ads could not identify the company by name, nor could they mention any specific products.

N.W. Ayer assigned Frances Gerety to the job, their only ad specialist who focused on women's products. She immediately proposed "to create a situation where almost every person pledging marriage feels compelled to acquire a diamond engagement ring." This became her mission and her mantra. It was during her design work for the campaign that she coined the slogan, "A Diamond is Forever." It was the start of a 25-year relationship, in which she wrote all of the company's advertising.

During the 1950s, as "Diamonds Are a Girl's Best Friend" was rising to its peak of popularity, Ayer's agents approached the major Hollywood studios, with offers to lend fabulous pieces of jewelry to their movie stars and starlets, provided they would wear them in films and at various high-profile social events. The quintessential cliché scene in movies of the 1950s showed the older, wealthy, powerful man, giving a glittering diamond bauble to the swooning young beauty. In a ritual erotic simulation, he would typically slip it on her finger, or stand behind her and place it around her neck.

This was a great deal for the studio heads, who had their stars under long-term contracts, and needed to keep them pampered and happy.

But, as Winston Churchill famously asserted, "Success is never final." And De Beers is now moving into its twilight years. Unable to control the sources of supply as before, and faced with the twin threats of a highly competitive market and stagnating interest in diamonds, the "alpha" company must now adapt to a role as just one of the herd. Its market share has declined to about 40 percent, and its marketing strategies have adapted to a different age. The heads of the Oppenheimer clan lost interest in the diamond monopoly, and sold the company to Anglo-American Corporation, a South African primary-industry conglomerate.

What remains to be seen is whether De Beers and the other companies in the diamond business can keep up the artificial perception of diamonds as rare, costly to produce and shape, and psychologically compelling.

There might come a day when people purchase diamond-based jewelry at prices they formerly associated with the teen-age fashion market. The future is certainly not certain.

According to *Forbes* magazine:

> But one thing, at least, has remained firmly established: the line "A Diamond Is Forever," which has appeared in every De Beers engagement ad since 1948. In 1999, two weeks before Frances Gerety died at the age of 83, Advertising Age named it the slogan of the century.

"Here's something to think about: How come you never see a headline like 'Psychic Wins Lottery'?"

~ *Jay Leno, American comedian*

PBI # 29: Maybe Molecules Have Minds?

Do molecules have minds? How far "down" does intelligence go? Organisms? Organs? Cells? Molecules?

Scientists have shown that stem cells can be "pluripotent," meaning that they can become virtually any kind of cells in the body.

What they haven't figured out so far is: what tells a new cell what kind of cell it's supposed to be? All cells contain exactly the same DNA, and nothing in the DNA codes for any particular kind of cell.

When a new cell develops in the liver, how does it "know" that it's supposed to become a liver cell and not, say, a skin cell? So far, no blueprint mechanism for cell identity has been found.

Some researchers posit the existence of a "morphogenic field," which is a hypothetical field of information that permeates all living structures. Supposedly this information field provides the formative data for the development of all new cells and organs. That might explain how a salamander can grow a brand new tail, identical to the original one that was chopped off.

So, where does the cell's knowledge reside?

"Money can buy you a fine dog, but only love can make him wag his tail."

~ *Kinky Friedman, Texas writer and activist*

Little Things Really Add Up

While we're preoccupied with reducing the use of fossil fuels and the attendant pollution, let's not forget some of the "small stuff" that makes a huge difference on a grand scale.

For example, China produces about 45 billion pairs of disposable chopsticks per year, and exports another 15 billion of them to Japan. This requires cutting down – and, one would hope, replacing – about 25 million trees per year.

Disposable plastic containers pile up in the environment at astonishing rates. Americans toss out an estimated 1500 empty plastic bottles *per second*. Plastic bags account for hundreds of millions of tons of durable waste, most in landfills. A remarkable amount of sun-decomposed plastic is accumulating in huge patches at the surface of the ocean.

Disposable diapers also deserve consideration. Industry statistics indicate that Americans use over 18 billion of them per year. Add consumption in other countries, and it adds up to about 25 billion.

Probably very few of the people who generate this vast tide of durable waste believe they're having a negative impact. "I'm only one person," goes the rationalization.

We might think of this attitude as the "snowflake exemption," after the comment by Stanislaw J. Lee:

"Each snowflake in an avalanche pleads its innocence."

Watch Your Language!

(Note: this item necessarily contains language that some readers might consider obscene. That's the whole point of the topic, but feel free to skip it if you prefer.)

"The way kids talk these days – it's appalling. They can't even speak a complete sentence."

"What's happening to this culture – this society? The TV shows, the movies, the songs, the news, blogs, emails – they're all degenerating to a common level of profanity and vulgarity."

Those of us who resent the increasingly coarse tone of the cultural conversation will just have to face the facts. And one big fact is that all human languages keep evolving over time, some further and faster than others.

That's either a good thing or a bad thing – take your choice.

Some of the words and expressions we commonly use today were once considered profane or vulgar. For example: "His partners screwed him out of a lot of money." A few decades ago, the slang verb "screw" generally referred to the physical act of intercourse, sometimes against the will of the person on the receiving end. But lately, even women and children use it freely as a general figure of speech, meaning that something has gone wrong – "It's all screwed up."

Another strong word that's moving up in the common vernacular is "suck." "You suck at tennis;" or, "Your table manners suck." The sexual connotation is fading out; even an inanimate object or an experience can "suck."

And the four-letter word that rhymes with suck is showing up in formerly forbidden places. Very few stand-up comics can get through more than a half-dozen sentences without inserting the adverb "fucking" for emphasis somewhere. Young women increasingly use it for aggressive emphasis in conversation. Those who are not quite sure have the option of using the milder form, "frigging."

In the media environment, the use of "fucking" seems to be spreading faster on screens than in print. Newspaper writers often substitute a cryptic version such as "f---ing" for the complete spelling, certain that almost all of their readers will know the meaning. In online news items, some sites spell it out and some encode it. A few of the more provocative outlets, such as motherjones.com, even spell it out in the article headlines or sub-heads.

Interestingly, the use of "fuck," as a transitive verb, is still much less respectable than the adverb form "fucking." Even in comedy clubs, a statement like "I fucked my girl friend" is considered much more vulgar – and often even intolerable – than "My girl friend and I get into an argument every fucking night."

And the ageless terms "shit" and "bullshit" are also progressing toward respectability – or at least out of the category of socially unacceptable profanity. As of this writing, most media sites seem to use the encrypted version, but the more aggressive ones spell it out in body text and even in headlines. It's not uncommon for a news item, especially an on-screen item, to quote some celebrity or politician as "dissing" another by referring to his or statement as "That's bullshit [or bull****]." And "crap," of course, has just about reached full respectability.

Another term that's almost acquired full respectability is "pissed off," or just "pissed." Motherjones.com, for example, uses it occasionally in article headlines, and many women seem to find it a useful shorthand reference to anger or annoyance.

But here's an interesting question. Why does our language – and almost every other human language – have a special sub-vocabulary for profanity? Why have a special collection of words, phrases, and figures of speech that are restricted from general use? What are the circumstances in which we're authorized to use them?

The people who study these things tell me that profanity is commonly associated with *aggression*, and the right to behave aggressively is associated with power and status. What's the difference between saying, "Every stock I ever invested in went down," and "Every fucking stock I ever invested in went down?" According to psychologists, the second version adds an element of aggression – as well as emphasis.

Looking at it that way, consider how differences in social status, authority, and physical dominance determine who's entitled to swear and who isn't.

222

In most cultures, adults forbid children to use profanity. This reinforces the child's subordinate social status and his or her lack of physical dominance. "Children should be seen, and not heard." And – we might add – they should talk nicely. It's not uncommon for parents to admonish children when they presume to swear in adult language. Overuse of profanity sometimes signals an extremely rebellious teen. American teenagers seem inordinately fond of the term "Oh, my God," contracted to "Omigod," or texted as "OMG." This vernacular use of the deity's identity seems to pass as their only allowed form of swearing, and maybe that's why they tend to use it constantly.

Males in almost all cultures tend to think of women who swear as not "ladylike," which generally translates to "not properly respectful or subservient to men." Compliant women typically characterize swearing behavior in the same way. "She swore like a sailor" sometimes conveys contempt and in some cases conveys respect or admiration.

As women in Western cultures become more confident in their economic and social status, and more assertive of their own interests, their use of profanity tends to increase. In effect, by invoking the privilege of using profanity, they reduce the power distance between males and themselves, and they typically expect males to accommodate the changes.

And, of course, formal authority confers the privilege of using profanity. The dominant figure in a power hierarchy – most often a male, but now increasingly female – typically has a greater right to act dominantly, and profanity is one of the signal systems of power.

When military officers assemble in a meeting room, their language typically starts out "clean." The ranking general is the one who gets to speak with "attitude," or to offer an off-color joke. The others can then partake of the privilege, provided that their level of expressed aggression doesn't exceed the chief's. Female senior officers and chief executives acquire the same rights, but may or not assert them, depending on their internal rule systems.

So, we'll probably be seeing more and more use of four-letter words and their cousins in Western cultures, as the general level of aggression rises; as the shock effect of profane language fades out; and as women increasingly assert their power in social and political hierarchies.

223

The elegance and beauty of language will certainly survive, in the custody of those who value it. And at the same time, the language of the commons will continue to evolve toward more practical purposes.

English is a Weird Language: # 2

How the hell did we ever get a word that's spelled "neighbor?"

If that's OK, shouldn't "labor" be spelled "leighbor?" Would a cavalry sword be a "seighbor?"

Should "wait" be spelled "weight?" No, that means something else.

Should "ate" be spelled "eight?" No, "eight" is a number.

"Rain?" No, "reign" means something else.

I'm getting a brain cramp . . .

The Most-Photographed City Sign in Europe?

Entering a charming little Austrian town, one sees:

Yep, that's the real name of a real town.

Is God Mentally Healthy?

God, as most western religious people define Him, seems like a pretty maladjusted guy.

According to popular teaching, we're supposed to fear him and love him at the same time. "We're God-fearing people." What kind of a claim to godly goodness is that? It sounds like the relationship an abused child might have with the abuser.

Also, according to the teaching, God is admittedly "a jealous god." He's emotionally insecure. He doesn't seem to have enough self-confidence, or belief in his all-powerful status, to be sure he'd win the competition with various other gods people might want to go with. Or, at least, that's what devout believers seem to believe about him.

He also plays favorites – not exactly a noble trait in a loving parent. "We're God's chosen people" apparently means that God has decided that all the other people are losers. "With God on our side, we'll defeat our enemies and win this war."

He's also moody, and he has a bad temper. He might decide to knock you off your bike one day, just for the fun (or the hell) of it. No reason given; you didn't do anything wrong. It's just "God's way," and you're not supposed to understand it or question it.

Hurricane? Earthquake? Plague? "It's God's will." Man, he must be big-time bored and short on fun things to do.

One of my fundamentalist friends admonishes me regularly that I'll go to Hell (big-time Hell, with a capital "H") if I don't start believing in his god.

My usual answer is, "I'll take my chances. If there is a God, I'm willing to bet she's a pretty nice person."

Just my take – your mileage may differ.

Don't Aim for the Moon

People love to say stuff like, "Shoot for the moon."

But that makes no sense.

When the astronauts went to the moon, they didn't aim their rocket ship at the moon – they aimed it at the place where the moon was going to be, allowing for the distance it would have moved while they were getting there.

Of course, I guess it's not very inspiring to say, "Calculate the celestial mechanics of the moon's orbit and follow a trajectory that minimizes the energy expended in achieving a rendezvous."

Yes, I realize that I sometimes make things more complicated than they need to be.

Readin', Writin', and . . .

Missippi's literacy program shows improvement

Let's see, I think it's "em, eye, crooked letter, crooked letter, eye . . ."

✪ ✪ ✪ ✪ ✪

"People should learn before they die,
what they're running from, and to, and why."

~ *James Thurber, American writer, cartoonist, & humorist*

✪ ✪ ✪ ✪ ✪

He Wanted to be Mayor for Life

Marion Barry got elected Mayor of Washington, D.C. three times – the third time just after he got out of prison. Apparently Washingtonians saw something in him to admire. Possibly it was his conceptual clarity, or maybe his articulate way of expressing himself. Some examples:

"The contagious people of Washington have stood firm against diversity during this long period of increment weather."

"I promise you a police car on every sidewalk."

"If you take out the killin's, Washington actually has a very very low crime rate."

"First, it was not a strip bar, it was an erotic club. And second, what can I say? I'm a night owl."

"I am clearly more popular than Reagan. I'm in my third term. Where's Reagan? Gone after two! Defeated by George Bush and Michael Dukakis, no less."

"People have criticized me because my security detail is larger than the President's. But you must ask yourself: are there more people who want to kill me than who want to kill the President? I can assure you there are."

"The brave men who died in Vietnam, more than 100 percent of which were black, were the ultimate sacrifice."

"I read a funny story about how the Republicans freed the slaves. The Republicans are the ones who created slavery by law in the 1600's. Abraham Lincoln freed the slaves and he was not a Republican."

"What right does Congress have to go around making laws just because they deem it necessary?"

✪ ✪ ✪ ✪ ✪

✪ ✪ ✪ ✪ ✪

Favorite Lame Joke # 12

Irish comedian Hal Roach tells of a couple who rented a small house on the outskirts of a village in southern Ireland. They noted that the house sat rather close to a railroad track, but the landlord assured them that very few trains ran along the track, and they weren't very noisy.

A few days after they moved in, the lady was at home while her husband was working at the factory. The first train that came along the track made a loud noise and rocked the whole house.

She called the landlord, with the intention of canceling the rental agreement. He offered to come over and evaluate her claims.

A few days later, when the next train was due, he paid a visit.

She told him, "The ruckus from the train is intolerable. It shakes the whole house; it actually knocks me out of the bed."

"Now, I think you're exaggerating, ma'am," he countered. "Let's just see how things are."

"Come in here," she demanded, "and lie on the bed – you'll see."

She lay down on one side of the bed, and he deposited himself on the other side.

Just then, the husband came in. Walking into the bedroom, he demanded, "Well, and what might be going on here?"

"You're probably not goin' to believe this," the landlord replied. "But we're waitin' for a train."

Need to Think? Take a Long Walk

There's nothing like a good long walk to clear your mind and help you get your ideas sorted out.

John Stewart, a somewhat eccentric British civil servant, left his job at the East India Company and decided to walk from Madras back home to London. And he took the long way. For over two decades – 1765 to 1790 – he traveled on foot through India, Persia, Abyssinia, Arabia, Africa, all of Europe, and into Russia.

This peripatetic adventure earned him the nickname "Walking Stewart." Historical accounts say little about his logistics – how he fed himself and how he sheltered – but one can assume he must have been in good condition by the time he reached London.

All of that walking and thinking paid off. Stewart joined the ranks of British intellectual society and began to write and lecture about his unique brand of spiritual philosophy. His contemporaries regarded him as a grand-scale thinker, despite his odd personality.

Stewart wrote more than 30 intellectual and philosophical treatises during the next three decades. He hung out with luminaries such as William Wordsworth and Thomas Paine. Always his own man, Stewart ended his life at age 72, with an overdose of *laudanum* – a medicinal tincture of opium.

228

A Credo for Living Sanely: Fifteen "Truths"

After 6-plus decades on the planet, I decided it would be a good idea to state, succinctly, what I believe I know about life. These 15 principles for living sanely are true for me.

1. I'm lovable, capable, and worthy – and I don't have to prove it.

2. My self-esteem is independent of external causes or consequences.

3. I think and act from the "place of cause" – I will not be a victim.

4. I'm responsible for the consequences of my choices.

5. There's no success or failure – we get what we program for.

6. Affirming and validating others affirms and validates me.

7. Giving love is the best way to get love.

8. I don't do guilt.

9. I don't do shame.

10. Life isn't a zero-sum game – more than one person can win.

11. I don't have to answer aggression with aggression.

12. I don't need to get revenge – I refocus my energy and move on.

13. I have the right to learn, make mistakes, and change my mind.

14. I keep my opinions on probation – open to new ideas and evidence.

15. I have no need – or right – to impose my "truth" on others.

This credo may be reproduced without restrictions. Please credit the source.

Download a printable poster version:

http://www.KarlAlbrecht.com/downloads/KarlAlbrecht-CredoForLivingSanely(WhatsTrueForMe).pdf

Introduction

If you've persevered this long, you might have enough energy left to read the typical author's diatribe: what I believe and why I wrote this book. Here goes, for whatever it's worth.

My website declares:

I believe that *ideas* are the ultimate form of wealth, whether we're talking about a business enterprise, a community, a social institution, a government, or a nation. Ideas are the *magical capital* that animates all other forms of capital.

Ideas move the world – the best and the worst of them. The nineteenth century writer Victor Hugo said,

> "There is one thing stronger than all the armies of the world; and that is an idea whose time has come."

The ideas we create, nurture, support, teach, and preach define us as a people. We *move forward* as a species when we honor and respect the rights of all human beings to do their own thinking. And we *regress* as a species when we try to silence, oppress, punish, or persecute those whose ideas do not fit with our comfortable story of reality.

I freely admit to being addicted to ideas. My heroes and mentors have always been the "big idea" people, whose lives testify to their commitment to open-mindedness, imagination, global thinking, curiosity, creativity, possibility thinking, tolerance, and the courage to innovate.

Charles Kettering, one of America's most prolific inventors, who became Vice President of General Motors and founded the Sloan-

Kettering Institute, believed that our culture *stifles* innovation rather than stimulates it. According to Kettering,

> "Human beings are so constituted as to see what is wrong with a new thing, not what is right. To verify this, you have only to submit a new idea to a committee. They will obliterate ninety percent of rightness for the sake of ten percent of wrongness. The possibilities a new idea opens up are not recognized, because not one [person] in a thousand has imagination."

My business colleagues sometimes describe me as a guy who's "constitutionally incapable of specializing in one thing per lifetime." They often say "His specialty seems to be the lack of a specialty." On most days, I take that as a rather high compliment – although it has made building a career somewhat more challenging than it otherwise might have been.

Science fiction writer and futurist Robert Heinlein said,

> "A human being should be able to change a diaper, plan an invasion, butcher a hog, conn a ship, design a building, write a sonnet, balance accounts, build a wall, set a bone, comfort the dying, take orders, give orders, cooperate, act alone, solve equations, analyze a new problem, program a computer, cook a tasty meal, fight efficiently, die gallantly. *Specialization is for insects.*"

I believe that intelligent, talented, and motivated people *can* do more than one thing well. When we turn our minds to new challenges – in a spirit of humility and willingness to learn – we might even outsmart the encamped experts who know what can't be done. The Zen master Shunryu Suzuki said,

> "In the beginner's mind there are many possibilities; in the expert's mind there are few. The most important thing an expert needs to learn is how to think like a beginner."

Big-idea thinking has always been in short supply, and we need it now more than ever.

Credits, Disclaimers, Et Cetera

The items in this collection of brain snacks come from three main sources: 1) stuff I think up; 2) stuff I get from other writers and thinkers, whom I identify as the sources when I know who they are; and 3) stuff from that mysterious "Unidentified Internet Source."

The third category reflects an unfortunate truth, namely that a lot of the novel, interesting, entertaining, useful, provocative stuff that circulates on the Internet gets disconnected from those who create it. Almost every day I get some kind of email message from a friend or colleague, forwarding a clever item or two, but I note that they're almost always anonymized. After eight or ten forwards, that clever little poem, joke, quiz, or factoid gets copied and pasted without giving credit to its originator. I've seen some of my own contributions cloned that way.

For those kinds of topics – many of which I've included in this collection – there's just no choice but to tip the hat anonymously to Mr. or Ms. Anonymous. I wish there were some way to give those people credit for what they create, but so far I haven't figured out how.

I've made a fairly diligent effort to verify or confirm the factual material I'm passing on. Some of those cute little Internet factoids turn out to be bogus, unsubstantiated, or invented; those I've dropped out. Others need a bit of correction. But in the end, I can't guarantee that every single assertion made in these pages is factually bulletproof. As they say, please don't consider anything in this book as medical advice, legal advice, or investment advice.

Whenever I've quoted directly from known books, news media, or other commercial publications, I've used short clips and identified the sources. This practice is generally accepted in Western countries as part of the "fair use" doctrine.

You've probably noticed that I'm a big fan of quotes and one-liners, typically offered by well-known historical figures. If you've also noticed that a particular quote or comment appears more than once, please think of that a matter of design, rather than incompetent proofreading. I want each brain snack to stand on its own, to the extent possible, and I'm assuming that many people who read this book might dip into it more or less at random. For that reason, I sometimes use a quote or an illustration more than once, so I don't need to depend on the assumption that the reader has already seen it in an earlier topic.

My style of prose tends to be upbeat, optimistic, sometimes whimsical, sometimes flippant, occasionally ironic, and often tongue-in-cheek. I haven't reached my spiritual plane of perfection yet, so once in a while I indulge in a bit of satire, sarcasm, or even a touch of scorn when I think somebody has it coming. I prefer to think of those occasional rants as adding a little dash of spice – both mental and emotional. We're all human, as they say.

Some of the rants and dissertation offered here first appeared in the blog that I've been writing for *Psychology Today* magazine for several years. If you like to read that sort of thing, then by all means bookmark <u>PsychologyToday.com/blog/brainsnacks</u>.

And if you want to contribute your own items to my bottomless toychest of brain snacks, please feel free to email them to me at <u>Brainsnacks@KarlAlbrecht.com</u>.

I hope you'll have as much fun reading this collection as I did writing it.

Best wishes – keep thinking . . .

The Beginning